Walkin The Dog

—ɯ—

By Darwin Demers

The Writers Guild Of America, west, Inc
Intellectual Property Registry
7000 West Third Street
August 22 2006

Walkin The Dog
by Darwin Demers

Printed in the United States of America

ISBN-13: 978-1-60034-991-1
IBSN-10: 1-60034-991-9

All Bible quotations are taken from the King James version
of the Bible.

Cover Art By Ryan Olson

www.xulonpress.com

To Lynn

[signature]

Happy Reading

This book is dedicated to Fred Bellis, a wonderful man and a true believer, my co-worker and my friend.

Table of Contents

—ɯ—

Chapter One - Nightmare 9

Chapter Two - Supernatural B.C. 29

Chapter Three - Enter the Dragon 43

Chapter Four - Greener Pastures 71

Chapter Five - New Realities 81

Chapter Six - Sing Another Prairie Tune 93

Chapter Seven - Go West Young Man, Again 97

Chapter Eight - To Farm Or Not To Farm 119

Chapter Nine - The Trial, Mistrial, and Aftermath 137

Chapter Ten - The Last Ten Years. 175

Chapter One

Nightmare!

—⟋⟍—

The silence of the forest surrounded me, as darkness fell like a blanket. Alone, I tried to slow the thoughts careening through my mind, smashing my convictions, destroying my ideals! What had I done..... More importantly..... What must I do now?

Everything seemed so surrealistic, as if I had just seen some shocking accident or scene which I couldn't get my mind around! I knew it had happened, I knew I was involved in it, yet some of what I had just seen.... Just couldn't be.... Couldn't be right!

The guy had been shot three times with a twelve gage shotgun, which had no effect whatsoever! How could that be.... Was I dreaming? I was there, I saw it, and yet what had I seen? I wasn't dreaming this, I couldn't be dreaming this.... I told myself .... I'm sitting in the dark out here in the forest..... Shivering here in the dark, in the forest, and I have a twelve gage shotgun in my hands. **It had definitely happened and I wasn't dreaming, so what was I going to do now?**

I fumbled in my jacket pocket for another shell and shoved it in the chamber of the shotgun. With my thumb on the trigger I turned the gun, and by turning my head was just able to touch the muzzle of the shotgun against my cheek. Could I squeeze the trigger? The barrel of the Remington Wingmaster seemed to be growing longer by the second, which prompted the thought that I'll probably wound myself and spend the rest of my life as a vegetable!Slowly I lowered the gun, set the safety to on, leaned the gun against a tree, and then stumbled six or seven steps through the dark, which by now was pitch black. I couldn't see my fingers an inch from my eyes, it was that dark! Finding a tree to lean against I crouched down, made myself as comfortable as possible and waited. It won't be too long I thought, they'll be coming for me, I may as well wait right here.

About forty-five minutes passed before I heard panting..... Like the panting of a dog as he goes about his business. For some reason I called out, " Is that the police?" The answer came quickly," Yes, it is." " Is that a dog I hear with you?" I quizzed. Again "Yes, it is." Is your dog on a leash?" I continued. Once more, "Yes, he is." " What do you want me to do?" I asked.The officer responded, " Are you armed?" " I placed the shotgun against a tree about 10 feet away, but in the dark I'm not sure where it is now." The officer spoke calmly, " Lie face down, with your hands behind your head and count out loud so I can locate you." I complied and within a minute or two my hands were gently cuffed behind my back.

Events moved rapidly from there as more R.C.M.P. officers filtered into the forest flashlight beams broken by the trees. I was taken into custody and brought from the forest where I was read my rights and placed in a police car. There were many policemen (perhaps fifteen) and cars, lights flashing, a helicopter high above it's searchlight on us, the dogs, and of course the media with their television cameras and lights everywhere.

The scene was extraordinary, like something out of a Hollywood movie, , as I was driven away from the site to the police station. The constable driving the vehicle was quiet and we said little to each other although later I was told I had cried out that I had ruined my life and the lives of my family. It must have seemed quite mundane to the constable; all in a day's work, so to speak. To me it was earth shattering, life changing, a never to be forgotten episode in my life! Here we were the two of us, in the same car, on our way to the same place but having two totally different experiences! As close as we were, physically, we couldn't have been further apart.

At the police station, my rights were read to me again, my personal effects were removed and logged, and I was placed in an observation cell. This cell was just across the hall from the guard's station in the jail. The guard's station had a large window in it facing the observation cell which also had a large window in it. People were interned here when the authorities were concerned that the prisoner may be suicidal. That's probably a good idea but just a tad embarrassing when you have to go to the bathroom. Every time I had to use the toilet in the cell, whoever was in the guard station could see me! Many female officers came and went from there and I did my thing as quickly as I could to avoid being seen.... But, how private could you be in a situation such as this?

My first conversation was with a Sergeant Tidsbury, of the Kelowna detachment of the R.C.M.P. He was sympathetic, knew how to put me at ease, got me a coffee, made me comfortable, read me my rights, exchanged pleasantries, such as discussing hockey, and personalized the conversation by telling me facts about himself, such as being from Lloydminister, Alberta. I was in fact being interrogated by a highly trained professional, skilled in gaining the confidence of his prisoner, and **I never knew the interrogation had already begun!**

After speaking with Sergeant Tidsbury, I was told that a Doctor Semrau would like to talk with me for a while, simply to ascertain my state of mind. I don't recall whether my approval was requested or required, but I would have agreed to talk to anyone willing to listen at that point anyway. I was extremely upset and emotionally unstable because of what had just happened. Everything I had been holding inside me for the past three years, had finally burst it's walls and came gushing out!

First Sergeant Tidsbury, then Doctor Semrau, and then Sergeant Tidsbury again, as I poured out my heart to them! Even though my rights had been read to me, I had shot my neighbor three times with a twelve gage shotgun, and the authorities had me and now I had to try and explain ... **Why!** Reflecting back on that night, I suppose part of the reason I didn't think the official interrogation had begun, was because no lawyer was provided. I mean every time my rights were read to me... while I was told I wasn't required to say anything and that I could call a lawyer if I wanted to.... They would just resume questioning me and didn't stop there saying something like here is a phone, you're in big trouble and you can or you should or you **better call a lawyer!**

Just prior to completing the evening's interrogation, Sargeant Tidsbury informed me he had just gotten word from the hospital that Steven Lee, the man I had shot was in no grave danger and would live! "Thank God, I cried, as a huge burden was lifted from off my shoulders! I wasn't a killer, and Steven Lee's soul wasn't going to be lost because of my actions! It wasn't just the relief of knowing the man I had shot would live but that somehow in my mind it seemed less serious!Every problem which had occurred over the three years between Lee and my family, culminating in the shooting, was now out of my hands! I no longer had to deal with Steven Lee or the trouble he caused, because for the time being I was in jail, and he was in the hospital.

It was approximately 5pm on January02,1995 when I was brought in to Kelowna R.C.M.P. detachment for questioning. At about 9pm I was finally returned to my cell where I curled up on the concrete bed exhausted and fell asleep. After a fitful night's sleep, I awoke to the sound of someone bringing me breakfast. I had a final interview with Sargeant Tidsbury after breakfast and was returned to my cell. At this point I had been allowed no visitors, nor was I informed that anyone had been turned away.

The next morning, after breakfast, I was cuffed, and ushered along with half a dozen other prisoners into a sheriff's van and driven to the courthouse where I made a brief appearance before a judge who informed me that I was being charged with attempted murder among other things and would be held in jail pending a bail application. Shortly thereafter I was returned to my cell.

Later that day, I was visited by my wife Carol and Dianne Roth, posing as my sister. Dianne was our close friend and tenant, who moved into our basement suite after her husband Doug, died from cancer. The Roths had attended the same church as us for fifteen years and we had been good friends. Following Doug's death Dianne decided to study nursing, sold her home to support herself while retraining and moved in with us.

The first thing Dianne said to me was, "Darwin don't worry, we'll get you out!" I tried not to cry, but I'm pretty sure I did a little, as I thought to myself she simply doesn't know what she's saying. While she tried to look as brave as Dianne, I could tell that Carol was still in a state of shock and disbelief! She was trying to be purposeful and efficient as she rattled off relevant information about the kids, family, work, etc; but I could tell she just wanted to cry and shout at me " What have you done!"

Instead she told me that our brother in law David Bush, had called from Kamloops as soon as he heard what had happened. David recommended a lawyer to Carol and asked if it would be alright to have him contact her. His lawyer friend's name was Brian Jackson, and they had grown up together in Trail, going right through school together. Carol had said it was ok and that after talking to Brian, he informed her I shouldn't talk to, **ANYONE** until I had first spoken to him! "Man, I thought, is he in for a surprise!"Carol informed me that Brian would be contacting me that day. She stated that few visitors were being allowed to see me and several close friends had already been turned away. This was news to me, but later I discovered that the police know how vulnerable a suspect is when first apprehended and they try to get everything they can from him before anyone has a chance to otherwise warn them of that fact.

Shortly after the girls left I was returned to an interview room and told to expect a call from a lawyer. When the call finally came it was from Brian Jackson in Vancouver. He told me he had been asked by my brother in law in Kamloops to contact me, and that he would represent me at my bail application if I wanted him to, and that we could discuss further plans after the bail application. I said that would be fine with me and he went on to ask me who I had talked to and what I had said.

Brian was shocked when he found out I had spoken to Sargeant Tidsbury for several hours as well as a psychiatrist, Doctor Semrau, who as it turned out was to be one of the expert witnesses for the Crown in their case against me at trial! Brian didn't understand why I hadn't remained silent until having spoken to a lawyer who would represent me first? I went on to explain as well as I could how I needed to tell someone what had happened. Brian wasn't happy though, that's for certain. Before ending the call he instructed me not to say anything else to anyone before he arrived in Kelowna.

Time passes very slowly in a jail cell when you're alone, so I was thankful when a guard offered me a few books to read. I even looked forward to the conversation during finger printing just to break the monotony. Although I wasn't allowed many visitors over the next few days my little sister Paula, got in as did several pastors from churches in the area. Paula gave me a "Get Out of Jail Free"card and I received several very uplifting cards and letters from co-workers and friends, which I stuck in the cell window.

One card which stood out from the rest came from a friend I had worked with, which had a picture on it showing a cowboy grasping his horse's reins,while the horse, standing on the edge of a precipice, looks down at his rider hanging on for dear life! Even the horse had a horrified look on his face! Below the picture was inscribed the message," Hang in There, Buddy". That card started me laughing which I did heartily for the next ten minutes. Thanks Wayne your card couldn't have come at a better time! Many a guard or constable would stop and look at those cards then leave with a grin on their face.~

"Daddy, is this what you did in the war?" I asked. " Sort of son. Only I flew a fighter plane, called a Spitfire, with guns in the wing." "Did it fly as fast as this airplane, Daddy?" " Much faster Darwin, they had to fly as fast as they could." " When will we see Mommy?" We'll be over our house in a few minutes son and you'll see mom waving to us on the back steps."

My dad had been a fighter pilot in the R.C.A.F.(Royal Canadian Air Force) in the Pacific theatre during the Second World War. Daddy was my hero even though I knew little about him aside from that fact and that now he and Uncle George owned the Empire Hotel in Meadow Lake, Saskatchewan. To me he was the best flier in the world!

" There's Mommy, now" Daddy shouted. " Wave to Mommy, Darwin, wave to Mommy!" and he banked the Cessna into a shallow dive down nearly to the roof top of our house below. "I see her Daddy, I see her!" I shouted as I laughed and squealed, "Hi, Mommy, Hi" and before I knew it, up, up, up, we climbed into the sky leaving Mommy far, far, away as we headed back to the field where our car was parked.~

Strange how your mind wanders when you're sitting in a jail cell. It's as if the mind simply becomes bored and decides to take a trip. My daydreaming episodes had always seemed to involve reliving past experiences I had found enjoyable. I don't know whether that has anything to do with being an optimist or a dreamer? I had little to do but read, think, sleep and cry, as I tried not to listen to some of the insults the prisoners made when a guard walked by. What a thankless job those guards have, being expected to tolerate the taunts and insults of prisoners who swore at them every chance they got.

The cell door opened and a Sargeant Tidsbury appeared, " A lawyer is here to see you Darwin," and out I went to an interview booth.

Mr. Brian Jackson was about forty-five to fifty years of age and maybe a hundred and eighty pounds. He had a full head of gray hair and was wearing jeans. There was a glass between us, as I sat down facing him, he introduced himself. " Hi, Darwin, Brian Jackson, I've just come from your home where I 've been visiting with Carol and the rest of your family, just getting to know them, taking a few notes, things like that." " Hi," I replied, not knowing quite what I was expected to say, or what was coming next.

" You know you're going to do time!" The words hit me like a brick, " I know," I choked, all the while hoping he was wrong. " I'll be visiting with the Crown's office shortly, your bail application will be this Friday, (it was Wednesday evening now). " I have a lot of work to get done and little time in which to complete it. I wanted to meet you, in person, let you know where we're at and to reiterate that you are under no obligation to say anything to the authorities, so please **don't** say anymore. I 've had a look at what you said to Tidsbury and Doctor Semrau, and I think we're alright, but please don't say anymore to anyone here. They are not your friends!" "Ok, Brian," I said. " I have to go now, Darwin," Brian said, " Hopefully we'll have you out of here on Friday", and with that we said our goodbyes and my first meeting with my lawyer was history.

Upon returning to my cell I flopped down and had a good cry as I thought about what Brian had said..... **I was going to do time....** which meant I'd lose my job and pension, and couldn't pay the bills, and wouldn't be able to support my family! I had just spoken to my lawyer, the guy I was depending on to get me out of here, and the first thing he tells me is.... **I'm going to do time!** The despair I felt at this moment was overwhelming! I drifted off to sleep...... ~

Ring...... Ring ..... I raced to the phone, " Hello, Darwin here," " Darwin, Paul Maneagre here, are you coming to the lake with us?" " You bet, I am, when are you leaving?" I asked as calmly as I could." We'll be leaving day after tomorrow," Paul said. " So if you can be at the house here around 8:30 am?" " I'll be there," I said, and hung up.I was so excited, I could barely contain myself as I asked mom and dad for permission . After a thorough grilling, they reluctantly gave their consent, knowing that Waskesiu was only seventy miles away. I would be living and working with the Maneagre family at their riding academy. Mr. and Mrs. Maneagre had three daughters, Paulette, Lillian, and Lorette, as well as a girl friend, Alice Benoit who also worked as guides. I loved horses and with all those girls to work with in a national park with a ton of fun things to do..... This would be my best summer yet!

Two days later we started freighting horses to Waskesiu from Prince Albert. We made five or six trips over the week, until we had fifty head of quarter horses, Welsh and Shetland ponies as well as a few donkeys at the riding academy. There was feed and tack to unload, and riding trails to be checked in preparation to opening for the public. We began doing trail rides almost immediately though while we continued doing all the chores in our spare time. After all paying customers were the reason we were here in the first place!

Waskesiu was the destination for many people because it was a national park which encompassed a huge lake and surrounded by a dense forest. There was a beautiful eighteen hole golf course located there, with tennis courts, dance halls, and a movie theater. Waskesiu was the "In" place to be during the summer! There were all the business owners and staff, catering to the tourist trade, in addition to administration and policing authorities, and all the maintenance people required to keep a town's infrastructure running smoothly.

Waskesiu Riding Academy had miles of trails winding through its forests on which to enjoy a horseback riding experience, and we were busy accommodating the riding public from 9:am til 9:pm. The trails were all named with wood signs such as Bear, Wolf and Crow Trail, and the horses got to know them very well. This often presented problems for the guides and the riders because the horses knew if a run was coming up. They also knew where a Trail intersected another Trail, and if it was deemed to be a shortcut back to the barn, the horse might take it on it's own and head for home by itself!

Many people don't have a lot of skills riding horses and go because they might enjoy trying something different, or perhaps they think it might be a great way to see the forest. We always had to be on the lookout for wildlife when we were on a ride. One day just after lunch we were out on large ride which required guides at the front and rear. I positioned myself at the rear and as the ride progressed I began to fall asleep. Suddenly I was flying through the air, and as my eyes blinked open I saw a cow moose and her calf go crashing right through our ride! Horses were bucking and riders were being thrown all over the place!

One hot afternoon just after lunch, Paulette and I were walking from the house to the barn when I spied a large winged ant on a tree stump by our path. Without thinking I quietly picked it up and threw it at her! As if the ant was a guided missile it landed right between her breasts, and she tore her halter top off, right in front of me! Paulette was well endowed, and I was riveted to the spot for what seemed an eternity, as she danced wildly her ponderous breasts bobbing everywhere. She was completely oblivious to me as she shook that halter top, focusing on the ant!

I spun around in my tracks, horrified at what I had done, wondering how I was going to get out of this predicament! As I stood there, blushing beet red, my back towards her, Paulette began to laugh, realizing how funny it all looked! What a relief it was as I quickly apologized, excused myself, and hurried off to find some work to do! It didn't take long before everyone at the riding academy had heard this story, and had a good laugh over that incident! Every evening after chores, we all got together for a hot chocolate and cinnamon toast in the kitchen. There wasn't a guide who didn't have a funny story to relate to those present and we always had a great laugh! That night was especially funny as one blushing little cowboy bore the brunt of the jokes from everyone! After mug up, we usually headed out for a movie or maybe roller skating, but that night we went to Johnny Bowers Place for a great teen dance.

Each guide had a favorite horse they rode for the summer. I got a lovely sorrel quarter horse mare with four white stockings and a white blaze on her face. She was called Cinda Blaze, and she was a joy to ride because of her smooth gait and responsiveness to neck reining. She really became my best friend for the summer because there was no one I spent more time with.

As much fun as it was to work there for a kid that was horse crazy, it was work. Up early, feed the horses, clean the barn, take dirty sawdust to the dump, get fresh load of sawdust, return to barn, get cleaned up, change, have breakfast, back to barn, groom horses, saddle and bridle horses for the first ride, then hit the trails til noon, feed and water horses, have lunch, back in saddle til 5:pm, feed and water horses, wash, eat supper, and back in saddle until dark, feed and water horses, put tack away, doctor saddle sores, and by 9:pm the rest of the night was yours!

There were always other chores to fill whatever spare time we had such as new roof shingles for the barn. I did lot's of driving to and from the sawdust pile and the dump in the old pickup, and I was only fourteen! Whenever I saw policeman I just pulled my cowboy hat lower and hoped he didn't look too closely. They knew the truck was from the riding academy and never once stopped me. By summer's end my legs were so bowed from those long hours in the saddle each day, there was no mistaking where I worked! All good things come to an end though, as did summer holidays and soon it was back to Prince Albert and school.~

"Time to go", said the guard as the cell door swung open and once again I was handcuffed and loaded into the sheriff's van and driven to the courthouse. It was Friday and time for my bail application to be heard. Our courthouse was brand new and state of the art, and the hallway which was prisoner proof led straight to the courtroom I was to make my appearance in. On a signal I was sent straight down the hallway to the prisoner's docket. As I entered the courtroom it was such a shock to see many of my family, relatives, and friends, that I hadn't seen in one place that I could remember, brought here waiting to see me, wanting to show their support for Carol and I. It was a very humbling and sobering experience for me, realizing that I was the reason they were here!

As the judge entered the court, the command," **All rise"** was shouted, and everyone present stood until the judge was seated. The proceedings consisted of a summation of the charges against me by the Crown Counsel. It was difficult for me to listen to the Crown Counsel as he summed up what had happened to bring us to this place. Finally the charges against me were read:

a) **attempt to commit murder contrary to section 239 of the Criminal Code of Canada,**
b) **discharging a firearm with intent to wound maim or disfigure contrary to section 244 of the Criminal Code of Canada,**
c **and using a firearm during the commission of an indictable offence contrary to section 85(1) (a) of the Criminal Code of Canada.**

When the Crown Counsel had finished, the judge asked for the Defense to present it's arguments as to why I should be granted bail.

Mr. Brian Jackson, cited his legal arguments, supplemented with precedent setting examples of why bail should be granted to me. He presented my behavioral record within the community prior to the shooting incident, as well as eighty letters of reference to be considered. The Crown did not oppose bail but asked only that I not be allowed to return to my home in Westbank and that I be restrained from being in the presence of the Lee family. After a brief recess ordered by Judge Klinger, to consider the evidence, court was reconvened, bail was granted and set at fifty thousand dollars!

My son-in -law, Calvin Duchesne, stepped forward immediately and provided the money! I recall thinking, **God bless you, Calvin, for assisting me in my hour of need!** Mr. Howard Archibald and Mr. Dwight Stutters, who attended the Westbank Bible Chapel also offered to provide my bail, and though grateful, I thought it best to keep it in the family and not inconvenience others.

We went to the office area in the courthouse and signed the bail papers and were free to leave the building. What a wonderful feeling it is to be outside after five days in a cell! My daughter Janice drove me over to my sister Paula's, in Kelowna. I wasn't allowed to return to the Westside of the Lake in Kelowna, known as Westbank, which had been my home for fifteen years! That was going to take some getting used to, but I could stay with Paula until I was able to find a more permanent place to live.Paula's suite was small, but at least my wife and kids could visit me here until I found something more suitable. How wonderful to be reunited with my children, family and friends at my sister's little place! Talk about emotion..... Everyone just had to have a good laugh and cry! Carol had so much to relate to me about what had transpired since my incarceration. She and Dianne had begun a telephone campaign to request letters of reference from as many of our family members, friends and coworkers as possible, in preparation for the bail hearing.

Our lawyer, Brian Jackson, had been amazed to see well over one hundred letters gathered within three days! In addition offers of help poured in from people we had lost contact with for a number of years! I was informed that we had been placed on the prayer chain of our local church. When everything seemed to be going against me, I prayed, and without fail I have always been better off for it. Had I greater faith, I should not have worried and fretted so much about my future, as so many people were praying for me and my family! Sinner that I am however, I really felt that I had gotten myself into this terrible predicament and I was going to have to get myself out!

Carol told me of all the expressions of sympathy our family was receiving, and that an old friend had called and wanted to see her as soon as possible. Jim Harder had been a good friend in Kitimat, back in 1969,and was now living in Kelowna. After seeing my news story on television he immediately called Carol and offered any assistance he could provide!Jim began by offering his home for us to use for several weeks as he and his wife Martha were just preparing to leave for a short two week holiday to Hawaii. This was such a wonderful gesture as my sister's place was simply too small to accommodate my family, especially overnight. Jim assured us that once he and Martha returned from Hawaii, he would stand with us throughout the ordeal we had to face! He went on to calmly reassure us that nothing would happen very quickly from here on in so far as the law was concerned.

So the Harders flew off to Hawaii and the Demers family moved into their home for two weeks. It was wonderful to be with all my children again as Carol and I began to make plans as to how we would function under the restraints of the court ordered bail. My immediate supervisor, Mr. Dave Story, was contacted and advised that I should like to return to work as soon as possible. I had last spoken to him just before leaving for Christmas holidays and of course he was as shocked as everyone else at what had happened. Now that I was out on bail and recognizing that I couldn't work in the Westbank area, Dave)said he would talk with senior management and see what accommodations the company would make for me. The company would probably have been much happier had I not been around, but here I was and they had to make some decisions concerning me!

After a few days it was decided that I would be brought inside the service center in Kelowna, where I would be as invisible to the public as possible. Of course the company didn't want the type of public relations I was getting via the media. One requirement the company insisted on was that a recognized member of the psychiatric profession must sign a statement clearing me to return to work.

Once again I met with Dr. Stanley Semrau for an interview and examination as he would determine if I was fit for work. He favored my request with his letter of recommendation to the company and the arrangements were made for me to return the following week. The prospects of returning to work were daunting, but I had a family to support. I reasoned the job would be therapeutic as well, even though I was quite nervous the day I was to return to work. I would be learning a new job, totally computerized, with many new people I didn't know. How would they react to me? What would they be thinking?

As I walked into the B.C.Tel. office building that Monday morning I felt that everyone was watching me. Certainly everyone had heard or seen the news on television and the newspapers and of course the gossip had traveled through the staff like wildfire! I was greeted by Dave Story who invited me into a room to introduce me to my new supervisor, Mr. Dave Pack. Upon entering the room I was greeted by several senior management people including, the manager Mr. Dennis Baker, who shook my hand and welcomed me back to work. Mr. Baker informed me that I would be going to a different department than originally planned as two of the women had expressed concern about working with me! However a petition had been circulated and of the fifty two people working in that department, **only those two were opposed to my being there!** I really had to fight back the tears when I was told of the support for me!

In order to avoid conflict local management decided to place me on the test desk. This was fine with me and I was only too happy to be back. While Mr. Baker told me about the support many people had expressed for me, I wasn't convinced that he was one of them. The decision to allow me to return to work had not been made locally but came from upper level management in Vancouver. There was little doubt in my mind that the company and the union had had some intense discussions concerning Darwin Demers, that I was not privy to! If management could have had their way I would have been down the road, the union had other ideas.

The Hardy Street telephone office housed approximately four hundred people of many different disciplines, such as operators, engineers, classified and management people all seemingly interested in getting a look at me but trying not to be obvious about it. Learning a new job in this environment wasn't going to be easy because I was so self conscious of being under constant scrutiny, even though most of my fellow workers were very helpful to me. I sensed a feeling of mistrust running through the building however, especially among the people that didn't know me. This was understandable under the circumstances, who could blame them? I was cognizant of this fact as I tried to learn the job and blend in as quietly as possible. To their credit most of the people there were prepared to give me a chance and make their judgments based on first hand observation.

I knew some of the people working in this building, and it wasn't unexpected that a large majority would harbor all kinds of doubts concerning me! I tried to imagine how I would have felt had I been in their positions. No, it wasn't going to be easy to convince anyone that I wasn't a hothead; a time bomb just waiting to explode! Each day I would come to work and in the eyes of many I would be on trial! I found myself trying to prove my innocence to my coworkers, which really wasn't possible!

Many jokes concerning my situation were made at times often to cheer me up. Everyone knew how serious this situation was and yet many wanted me to know they empathized with me and so the jokes were received in the spirit with which they were given. I was very thankful for the words of encouragement, for the wishes of good fortune, for the prayers, for the jokes and joviality expressed solely to raise my spirits! In some cases people I had known and worked with for many years now avoided me like the plague! Perhaps they didn't know how to deal with a bad situation and would eventually come around. I made every excuse for them at first, but gradually I had to face the reality that we were going to lose friends. After listening to the news many of these people had already decided the case. Rather than wait for a trial; rather than accept that a person is innocent until proven guilty; rather than investigate for themselves or wait for the facts of the case to be investigated by the authorities; they simply took the quick way out and judged me **Guilty!** I don't blame them, in fact snap judgments had always been a trait of mine. There's truth to the saying **"As ye judge, so shall ye be judged"**

It really hurt to face open rejection and in some cases hostility from people who had in the past been friendly! Unfortunately some of these people were professing Christians! I wondered how they could be so unforgiving when they themselves had been forgiven their wrongdoings! Too many Christians do not exhibit that one characteristic which should mark the follower of Christ...... **forgiveness!**

As I write this book I am tempted to deal with specific stories of some of the deep hurt my wife and I experienced at the hands of people who had portrayed themselves as close friends. When friends of twenty years begin making excuses about why they didn't stop to visit when passing through town. When relatives that used to visit regularly suddenly stopped, without explanation; It hurt us deeply, but we have come to accept it!Many times I wanted to take them to task for abandoning us in our time of need, but then I would think what would be accomplished anyway? These people would probably deny to themselves as well as everyone else that they were ever really close friends of ours.As difficult as it was for us, Carol and I had to resign ourselves to this new reality and simply let them go.

One of the realities with which I had to deal was that I had been instructed to say nothing about the case to anyone, by my legal counsel. While Lee was in fact running off at the mouth to anyone who would listen, I was to say nothing.

The media saw Steven Lee as the victim and did their best to portray him that way. I was the perpetrator of a horrendous act against Lee and society. I had gone after him with a gun and I must answer for it! Who can blame anyone that didn't know the story for wondering at my guilt and initially siding with Lee? While some people knew the truth most didn't and I'm telling you that the media rarely gives the public the truth, the whole truth, and nothing but the truth. Anyone who has had dealings with the news media must realize that I'm stating the obvious here. My dad used to say, **" Don't believe anything you hear, and only half of what you see".**

While I was getting settled in my new job and trying to find a more permanent residence in Kelowna, the police were conducting their investigation in Westbank. Lee was back home within ten days and if things were bad before the shooting they were even more tense for my wife and kids now! He paraded back and forth in front of Carol and the kids every chance he got, letting them know he was watching their every move. My family had been terrified of this man when I was at home to protect them, but now I wasn't permitted to come home at all!

It seemed that the media had a news release on this story every week and it was clear they would follow it to it's conclusion. The only problem was that only Lee's side of the story was being told while I was being vilified publicly. Lee wanted everyone to think that the problems had begun simply as trouble between kids. To an unknowing public, this seemed plausible, when in reality it was Steven Lee who had been the instigator of the trouble all along! Not long after the police began their investigation, they concluded that he was a **"neighborhood bully"**!~

Chapter Two

Supernatural B.C.

—ᴧᴧᴧ—

It felt good to be coming back to B.C. for so many reasons! Maybe it was the sense of freedom we were experiencing at being off the farm; or the great fresh mountain air; or perhaps it was a feeling of coming home to the province we had been married and spent most of our married lives in..... maybe it was for all of these reasons. As we crossed the Alberta- B.C. border and headed down towards Revelstoke.... Sicamous.... Vernon, it got warmer and warmer. the season seemed to be moving backwards hour by hour towards midsummer again! Feelings of jubilation flooded over us, as we approached Kelowna, and the Okanagan Valley.

We crossed the beautiful "Okanagan Lake" and headed the further twelve kilometers to Westbank. The duplex we had rented prior to coming was waiting and we spent the next few days getting settled in. We got our furniture unloaded between telephone calls and visiting with Carol's family. Carol's mother, father, and youngest sister(Darlene) lived in Westbank. A younger brother(David) lived in Kelowna and worked with her father in the construction business. Still another sister(Elizabeth) lived between Westbank and Vernon on the West side of the lake with her husband David Bush and their two children Christopher and Jennifer. Elizabeth did the books for her father's construction business.

Westbank was a lovely little town, situated in the heart of orchard country, overlooking Okanagan Lake. Located just twelve kilometers from Kelowna it was close enough to be a suburb of Kelowna and yet distinct enough to have it's own post office, parks, and telephone office.After settling in we drove down to Peachland where we put our feet in the water and drank in the scenery of the gorgeous Okanagan Valley! I'm not exaggerating when I say we thought <u>we'd died and gone to Heaven!</u> Each province in this wonderful country of ours has it's own particular beauty, from the prairie we had left, to the orchard area around a lake, surrounded by mountains, with a moderate climate where we'd come.

Even here I would have to earn a living and I resolved I would set about that task the following week. I decided to begin in Westbank at the local B.C.Tel office where my first contact was the local Installation and Repair foreman, Mr. Bill Tams.We had a brief chat and Bill finally said, " **<u>I don't want to hurt your feelings Darwin, but you don't have a snowball's hope in hell of getting back on with the phone company</u>**"! I felt depressed, but thanked him for his candor and headed across the lake to talk with some of the telephone contacts Bill had suggested I see. After a brief interview with a senior manager I was told I would have to go to Vernon for an application and interview with the human resources department. I was hoping they weren't going to give me the runaround until I got tired and gave up.

I resolved that I would drive to Vernon the next day anyway and made an appointment with human resources in Vernon. Mona Hoy interviewed me and scheduled testing to ascertain my experience, while promising to explore any opportunities there might be for me in the area. It became apparent that this procedure would be fairly lengthy before any decision was made concerning me. In the meantime I decided to look for work elsewhere and secured a job in Kelowna, doing piece work for a cable t.v. contractor. I did installs in the Westbank area and picked up a nice job through the contractor doing installs for Penticton Cable for a month. They supplied my van and tools, but it was still piece work with no benefits, unless I got on steady.

Finally I got a call from B.C. Tel. with an offer of work in Salmon Arm. This sounds brazen, but after talking to Mona, I decided to wait for something closer to Kelowna to come along. I did say to her that if it meant I was going to lose a job for not moving to please let me know and I would consider it. The very next week she called and offered me a job in Vernon as an installer repairman. This time I jumped at the opportunity and hired on with the telephone company..... for the third time!The job in Vernon was full time, but as a temporary employee. While this wasn't exactly what I wanted, I had my feet in the door and was building seniority and I could bid on any full time positions which became available. It felt very good to be doing my old familiar type of work once more, especially in a much milder climate than the one we had left in Saskatchewan!

For the first three months I commuted back and forth from Westbank to Vernon,a distance of some forty miles. As this involved two full hours of driving each day, we decided to move to Vernon, over the Christmas holidays. My mom, dad and little sister, Paula moved to Vernon from Quesnel because Dad was looking for a milder climate to retire to. I think he just wanted to be closer to us and was too shy to admit it.Dad and I had been planning to pool our resources and build a home with a nice suite in it for them. He liked the idea that we could keep a watchful eye on Paula, while he and mom wintered in the southern states. For the time being however we were living across from each other on beautiful Kalamalka Lake in Vernon's Coldstream area, in houses we had rented.

We spent a mild winter in Vernon when the company offered me full time employment in of all places, Westbank, and I jumped at the chance! When I reported to the I&R Supervisor there everyone laughed as I shook hands with Bill Tams and said, **"Hi Bill, just call me Snowball!"** What a strange way to wind up back in the town we had moved to when we first came back to B.C. and working for the telephone company in the first place I had gone to try to get a job! Maybe it was just coincidence, I'm not sure..... maybe someone was trying to teach me a lesson?

I had finally landed a full time job with an excellent company in a highly desirable location! We purchased a new home in Westbank with an unfinished basement which dad and I set about developing. Carol's father and brother helped us, and after a month's hard work it was ready for occupancy. Carol, the kids and myself moved in upstairs, and mom, dad, and Paula took the basement suite as we settled into our new home. We were invited to a small church in Westbank and eventually got around to attending. The people were so friendly that it wasn't long before the Demers family became a part of the "Westbank Bible Chapel" family(a brethern assembly).

The Bible Chapel became our second home, not just a place to go for an hour on Sunday. We celebrated the accomplishments of our young people when they were baptized or graduated from high school. We rejoiced with them as they came of age and married and began new families. As babies came the new mothers had all the support they required from the many mothers attending the Chapel.There was support within the "Assembly" for everyone in need. When a death occurred, comfort and assistance were provided for the loved ones left behind. The Church's attitude was to assist those in need, which we believed was real Christianity, in action. The gospel was preached, but more importantly, the gospel was lived. Our little church ministered to the Demers family as it grew.

Our chapel supported a bible camp, by the name of "Morning Star Bible Camp" located up in the Glenrosa subdivision of Westbank. Each summer many youth, teen, and family camps were held there". Going to camp for part of summer vacation was fun and made for some wonderful memories. Singing, sports, games, crafts, and making new friends, were all part of the experience. Loving people staffed the camp as counselors, cooks, sports leaders, music and craft instructors, cleanup personnel, and ministers all under the direction of the camp director.

The love of the workers shone through, as people gave of their time and talent, working unselfishly for the weekly summer camps! Carol did crafts at camp, while I served as a musician and counselor many times over the years. Giving up a week's holidays to work at a bible camp probably seems at first glance to be anything but a holiday! If you were to ask any worker, they would tell you that they inevitably received far more from camp than they ever gave!

Morning Star Bible Camp had seventeen acres of forested hills on which to develop their camp facilities. The camp like the church, was **a work in progress**, much as we are! Nothing is perfect, point in fact...... the day I walked into that church it became imperfect.It's important to understand that all Christians are sinners, but their faith is in the "Sinless One". We believe that Jesus has paid the penalty for sin and opened the door to heaven for all who put their faith in him." He is the lamb of God who takes away the sin of the World! Christians are no better than anyone else, but we believe we are forgiven by the perfectly acceptable price exacted on the Messiah! If I hope to be saved by my own actions, I know that I am hopelessly lost! Our faith, our hope, our trust, is in **Jesus Christ!**

It's an important lesson to learn in life that we may be wrong! Reflecting on my life I realize how many times I have been wrong..... more than I care to remember! Certainly my views, ideas and opinions have changed or been modified over the years. On reflection, the insight of **hindsight** has made me much wiser! No man is an island, and the decisions I've made and the conclusions I've reached have affected many others including family, friends and foes.

The church and camp became an integral part of the Demers family as it continued to grow, and grow it did! Two more boys, Matthew and Phillip,(my redheads) and two girls Lesley and Lori, were added over the next eleven years,(I believe it was the water).Whatever the cause we were now a family of ten, with Mom, Dad, and my youngest sister living downstairs, so space was always at a premium. Speaking for myself though, I must say I loved every moment and the memories will remain with me always. We have thousands of pictures which have preserved many of the wonderful family times, but most of them are preserved in our minds..... each person remembering what was most important to them! How wonderful it is when we have a get together on some special occasion and while building new memories get the opportunity to relive and rejoice over many of the old ones!

B.C.Tel. was a good company to work for and was always more than fair to me. The company paid well, supplied all the training, and offered many opportunities for advancement! No doubt, the union was responsible for many privileges we enjoyed there, but it was a great place to work, and I have heard that for a long period of time our company was considered to be one of the top one hundred companies in Canada!

Carol's dad had a small construction company which operated out of Westbank. He had a couple of carpenters working for him, including his son, David, and a daughter who looked after the books. He hired sub trades based on the size of jobs he had to do. Tom Fusick, was a very hard working, talented builder, from the old school! He wasn't sophisticated, or well educated, and he often made deals on a handshake. While this may be a commendable quality in one sense, it is a serious fault in business, especially in this day and age! An ironclad legal contract often spells the difference between success and failure in today's business world! I recall the new cars, boats and homes which were all lost when business customers refused to pay their bills which contributed to Tom's bankruptcy! He showed me over two hundred thousand dollars owed him, which he was never able to collect! What a sad world this is, when a man's future can be so adversely affected by his misplaced trust in dishonorable people. There is a lesson here for all of us, but wouldn't the world be a better place if it was a lesson we didn't have to learn?

My dad had a saying (not original), **"There but for the grace of God, go I"**! Many times throughout my life I've reflected on this pearl of wisdom and have come to realize how true it is. Why am I not blind? Why was Christopher Reeves crippled? Why are we so fortunate to be born in one of the best countries on earth? I could go on, but why belabor the point ? We don't necessarily deserve the good fortune we enjoy in our lives, which could more accurately be called **blessings!** Imagine sitting in a card game and being dealt a perfect hand by the dealer! We would all be fairly excited wouldn't we! The point is, many of us have a great **deal** to be thankful for, which should be reflected in our attitude and behavior. My father was a thankful man regardless of the cards he was dealt. He returned from the war in the Pacific, a thankful man! Frank, a co-worker once asked me why I was always so happy? He had much more than me, and yet didn't seem content. I have to say, I don't believe that happiness is a purchasable commodity! Some will say; Money might not buy happiness, but poverty doesn't buy it either! or perhaps; Money might not buy happiness, but it buys a nice substitute! and in a way, they are right, but that isn't the whole story! There is no substitute for a satisfied mind!

St. Paul said it best..... " For I have learned in whatsoever state I am, therewith to be content."

Many rich and famous people seem very unhappy with their lives. I wonder if they really see the big picture; if they really know how fleeting life is and what follows?Happiness to me is a state of mind, that begins each day with a thankfulness to God, for the gift of life! Health of body and of mind are two contributing factors to the quality of a person's life. Love of family and friends is also important, and can compensate for much of what we lack in other areas.

There were nine guys working out of the Westbank C.O.(central office). We maintained telecommunications on the West side of the lake from Vernon to Summerland, but could be called on to go anywhere in the valley if necessary. We were a tightly knit little crew, who worked and often played together. Just across the lake in Kelowna were over four hundred employees, but they seemed a world apart from us and we had a tendency to do things our own way on the Westside. We had our own headquarters and work and holiday schedule which gave us a certain independence from telephone people in Kelowna!

While Carol and I hadn't planned on having so many children, it happened so slowly and naturally over the years that it was barely noticeable! One day I gazed around the table and realized that all ten chairs were full! Carol was extremely competent as a mother and homemaker, making everything look so easy, when it really wasn't. She was born to be a mother, and should have received an award for her life's dedication to the task of raising those children! Our family was a going concern with school and the various activities of each child clamoring for attention. Without a husband and wife, united in purpose, philosophy, and love, it wouldn't have been so enjoyable. Just providing the necessities of life can be a daunting task! We were up for it though and while we weren't perfect parents by any means, judging by the way the kids turned out, we're satisfied with the job we did, and I think they are as well.

Growing up in a large family has it's pluses and minuses which our children learned early on. Clothes weren't discarded because of style, but only when they wore out. Hand me downs were an accepted fact of each child's life, whether they came from siblings or relatives. When new clothes had to be purchased, functionality and cost rather than designer labels were the overriding factors to be considered. We ate well, but economized by buying bulk, using coupons, having a garden, taking advantage of sales, and staying with cheaper brands. We either picked or purchased fresh fruit when in season and then canned our own preserves. A fall sale of bulk produce where I could get 500 lbs. of potatoes at .10/lb. or carrots and onions always gave me a deep sense of satisfaction when the cold room was fully stocked, for winter.

My sister, Paula, graduated and eventually moved to Vancouver where she went to work for a law firm. Mom and Dad missed her very much, but thankfully our kids were there to keep grandma and grandpa busy! One of my folks pleasures was snow birding in Mexico and Arizona with friends during the winter. They also managed a trip one summer with Jeanette and Robert Semchuck,(mom's sister and brother in law) across Canada, visiting relatives in Quebec and P.E.I.

Every family must endure the traumas of life and ours was no different! Extremely traumatic for us was when my dad was diagnosed with throat cancer! Dad went to Vancouver, for a second opinion and when he called to tell me that his larynx was going to be removed the next day, it was devastating! Dad said that this was the last time he would be able to talk to me, so it was a very emotional moment for both of us!

We were so happy to see dad when he returned a few days later, not realizing that all that had been accomplished was to buy him some time. Frank, a co-worker, informed me rather bluntly of this fact, and I confess it shocked me, as I struggled with the reality that my father was dying! During the eight months following the operation dad went from 220 pounds to approximately 98 pounds! Dad did teach me one very important thing after coming home, even though he couldn't talk..... **Dad taught me how to die!** Never once did he complain to me, about his condition! One day while sitting out on the deck sunning ourselves I asked, "Dad, how do you feel about dying"? He wrote on his slate board simply, " It's part of living"! He had obviously spent some time thinking this through as his answer was short and concise!

While dad took his impending death with little apparent emotion, I in fact did not! Towards the end of his life I found it difficult and eventually impossible to visit him without breaking down, as the cancer progressed! Carol was considerate throughout his illness, as she would go down and read to him from the bible. He really got a great deal of comfort from these times and it gave mom a chance to go out and play bridge or just visit with a few friends.All our kids, had to come to terms with the fact that grandpa was dying. Some took it harder than others, and Mark seemed to be the most intensely affected. Life has it's way of teaching us all certain lessons however, and death forces itself on each of us with a finality all it's own. My father died in August of 1989! Dad was the original Archie Bunker, very tenderhearted even though he pretended to be just the opposite! I loved him very much and will miss him always.

While there were adjustments made in mother's life, she was grateful to have family upstairs for support and comfort. Carol took mom shopping and had her eat with us, often. Janice moved downstairs to keep her grandmother company and I suspect also to have a bedroom to herself at last (She had been sharing with three of her sisters)! Along with family and church friends , mom had some great bridge partners, so even though her life partner was gone she wasn't left completely alone. We were all able to comfort each other at the loss of the Patriarh, who had been so important to us all for so long!

Karyn graduated, and over her objections, we managed to persuade her to attend the " Baptist Leadership Training School"(B.L.T.S.) in Calgary for one year! She had been home educated for grades ten, eleven, twelve, and we thought it best for her to spend at least one year away from the family and Kelowna! Carol had attended B.L.T.S. for a year after her grade twelve and thought the experience would be good for Karyn as well.We had an ulterior motive for sending Karyn away to Calgary however which had more to do with a young man than either of us cared to admit! Truthfully though we both wanted her to see some of the world and get just a little life experience before she wound up married and not even dry behind the ears! She went obediently, but while she tried to make the best of it, her heart was never really in attending B.L. This was her mother's dream..... not Karyn's.

Calvin Duchesne, had taken an interest in Karyn, and was in Calgary at least twice a month, visiting and looking after his love interest. No way was he going to allow any young fellow at B.L. any chances with this girl.Calvin was twelve years older than Karyn, and although he was a very nice man, he was definitely a man and this really intimidated everyone at B.L.T.S.! The age difference between Karyn and Calvin really concerned Carol and I as parents for many obvious reasons, not the least of which Karyn had never dated before and it just took us so completely by surprise! I suppose that's life,though isn't it?As parents we are not prepared for the many situations which life brings our way and this was the case with our eldest daughter who was just coming of age. As soon as she finished the year at B.L.T.S. Karyn returned to Kelowna and after securing a job at a local insurance company, she and her sister Janice moved into a small basement suite in Westbank. The birds were starting to leave the nest.

It wasn't long before Karyn and Calvin announced their intention to marry and requested our approval. Carol and I had no life experience to draw on, to help us with this situation. Thanks to Spencer Tracy and Katherine Hepburn, in "Guess Who's Coming to Dinner", we decided to give the " Good Housekeeping" stamp of approval. We figured the two of them would have enough difficulties together, so we would give them all the help and understanding we could muster!

We had to trust their judgment that the age difference wasn't the predominant factor which would determine the success or failure of their marriage! They felt that common interests, philosophy, religion, and a need for each other, had to take preference over age. Sixteen years and four beautiful daughters later, Carol and I still have our fingers crossed!

Shortly thereafter, Janice's boyfriend, Murray, asked for her hand in marriage! We were overjoyed at what we thought would be a great match in everyway! They were the same age, attended the same church and seemed to share a lot of interests together. They were two beautiful people. Murray was the youngest of four boys and had two sisters as well. He always had time to play hockey with Janice's younger brothers and I think she really saw this as evidence that he would be a great father! Murray had a good job working at Gorman's Mill, the same mill that employed Calvin and many of the working males in Westbank. Janice and Murray's marriage ended in divorce two and a half years later! We were devastated by the failure of a union we had thought was ideal in every respect! The lesson here is when it comes to affairs of the heart there are no absolutes! It really takes two people to make a marriage work but only one to break it!

Mom had been planning to visit the Harmans (my sister and family), as well as her sister Jeanette, in Saskatoon, for quite some time. She hadn't been feeling all that well, but decided to go anyway, I'm not sure why? The day before she left for Saskatoon, she hosted a bridge tournament, and flew out the next day. I never saw my mother again.....

!Mom actually got sick on the plane and the Harmans took her from the airport straight to the hospital! She died in the hospital in Saskatoon within three weeks on July 07, 1992! She had that damnable cancer and to the best of our knowledge no one ever knew until she was diagnosed in Saskatoon! We had her cremated and the ashes returned for the funeral in Westbank, where she was laid to rest in the cemetery alongside dad!

My mother was one of the great loves of my life! She was an eternal optimist who spread joy wherever she went! Mom had the enviable quality of making people feel loved and accepted for which she was much admired! She had a tremendous sense of humour and loved to make people laugh! Many people, both in and out of the family, tolerated dad but, loved mom! It was kind of an Archie and Edith thing to put it in perspective. We had a wonderful mother and grandmother, a blessed gift from God, whose light will forever shine in our hearts!

We were only too happy when our friend, Dianne moved into mom's suite. It meant extra revenue for us which we could really use with a family the size of ours. Carol and Dianne loved to do crafts together and would often set up a booth at craft fairs to display their wares. Dianne enjoyed our family as much as we enjoyed having her with us. She became a sister to Carol, an aunt to our children and a member of our family.I admired Dianne very much for the way she handled adversity in her life. After losing her husband at the age of thirty eight to cancer, she pulled up her socks and began a course in nursing while continuing to support her family by working in a clothing store! Shortly after moving into our home she graduated and began her career as a registered nurse at Kelowna General Hospital.

Success isn't measured by the position we attain in life, but rather the obstacles we must overcome in attaining that position! By every scale one might care to use, Dianne was a successful woman. She volunteered time at the bible camp each summer as a counselor and was an optimistic influence on everyone who knew her and an inspiration to the Demers family!~

Chapter Three

Enter The Dragon!

—∿∿—

Steven Lee, entered our lives during the spring of 1992, when he purchased the house next door from the Dunns. We didn't suspect anything out of the ordinary as the Lee family was comprised of a mom and dad and a son and daughter..... at first glance a normal family in every way.It wasn't long before Mr. Lee made his first trip over to our home, while I was at work and complained about our boys not playing with his son Troy. He then went on to tell Carol that he hoped this wasn't going to become a big problem. This was the beginning of an increasing succession of visits by the man to our home, where he complained vociferously about the behavior of our boys.

One evening our oldest son David, just fifteen years of age was out on our deck looking out at the lake when I over-heard shouting going on, and went to investigate. There was Steven Lee standing on his deck swearing at my son! As soon as I came out he disappeared into his house. I asked David what was going on and he replied that he didn't know what was going on or why Lee had come out and started hollering at him!Of course this didn't ring true to me and made no sense whatsoever. I must say right there and then that a chill went right through me! **A normal man doesn't pick on children and he doesn't stand on his deck cursing at his neighbor's kids..... period!**

David was crying to his mother and the two of them decided to go over to talk with Steven Lee to find out what he was upset about and to see if they could resolve the problem! What an exercise in futility that proved to be! When confronted Mr. Lee began a foul mouth diatribe of groundless accusations against virtually every member of the Demers family. In this particular instance Mr. Lee was most concerned about a disparaging remark, ascribed to David, made about the Lee's dog (a beautiful boxer). Carol asked David if in fact he had made the particular remark to which he responded he had not. When pressed Lee confessed that he hadn't heard David say anything first hand, but that his son Troy had. At this point Carol insisted that since this story had sparked so much anger in Mr. Lee that it was only fair that Troy come to the door and tell what he knew. Lee reluctantly called his son and asked him to recount his story to all present.

Troy sheepishly admitted that it wasn't David who had in fact made the remark, but rather one of the boys who had been playing with David. When this came out Carol asked that Lee apologize to David for swearing at him and for wrongly accusing him, which he grudgingly did. Lee then went on to make it clear that Carol who was a noon hour supervisor at the kids school had better not let this affect her conduct or responsibility towards the Lee children or **he would have her job!**Then he proceeded to lecture her on having too many children which she obviously couldn't handle. Carol was told that we didn't own the street; that Lee's kids could play wherever they wanted; followed by a host of unrelated offensive and insulting remarks made by Lee. It ended with him telling David and Carol to get the hell off his property, which they promptly did!

We just couldn't understand the man's behavior or attitude on anything, but as time progressed it became evident that we had been singled out for special treatment from Mr. Steven Lee! Carol to her credit as a Christian added Steven Lee and his family to her list of people to pray for, and we resolved to do our best to peacefully coexist with them. We instructed our kids to play as nicely and fairly with the Lee kids as they could which seemed to work for awhile, as Shiela their daughter started coming over to visit with our daughters. Eventually back Mr. Lee would come swearing and cursing at Carol that our boys were causing problems for his son, Troy. When we talked with our boys about these incidents they invariably replied that it was Mr. Lee who wouldn't leave them alone! Rather than let the kids be kids and play their kid games, Lee was always watching, as if he was the referee and all the neighborhood kids had better mind him!

Lee called himself a landscaper, but in reality what he did was to mow lawns and trim hedges, basically things any fourteen year old could do, but at least it was honest work. This meant that he was at home many times during the day which gave him ample time to keep an eye on our family.... a job he relished! One could argue that he was just overprotective of his only son and who could blame him with four boys living next door, who perhaps were giving his boy a tough time? **I half believed the man myself for a period of time.** Boys would be boys and ours were far from perfect!

Gradually though I came to understand what my boys were saying about Mr. Lee. He was a bully who enjoyed throwing his weight around the neighborhood. Lee picked on kids, not just the Demers kids. There were a half dozen families in the area with boys who had been bullied by Steven Lee! The Frasers, Bakers, Seversons, and Harveys had all incurred the wrath of Steven Lee at different times for little or no reason. I knew many of these kids and without exception they were good children. If they did anything to

Troy Lee at all it was most likely in retaliation for Troy's father constantly picking on them. Still there is a tendency to take the word of an adult over that of kids in a situation such as this and **I didn't for one minute believe our kids were totally innocent in all of this!**

Finally Carol and I decided that our kids should make every effort to avoid Mr. Lee that was reasonable! They were instructed to go in the opposite direction whenever they saw him and they were not to play with Troy as they couldn't seem to get along, and the play inevitably led to trouble for all concerned. We even made the kids avoid playing in the portion of our yard which bordered the Lee property! This only seemed to infuriate Lee further as he saw it as a form of rejection and disrespect for him. How do you appease a man who picks on children, cursing and swearing at them and their mothers? We taught our children to respect adult authority and to speak politely to people, yet this so called adult was always hollering and swearing at them and no one could really understand how to deal with him! In actual fact everyone was scared of him, which he seemed to thrive on.

Mr. Steven Lee didn't care who he offended with his insults, his cursing or his offensive gestures. Some of our kids were as young as four and six years old but he would use every foul word he could think of whenever it suited him with no regard for their innocence whatsoever! We simply couldn't understand behaviour such as this from a neighbour who appeared to be normal and had two children of his own! None of us had ever experienced anything like this in our lives before. Dianne suggested baking buns and taking them over to try and be friendly and maybe this would somehow overcome the feelings of hostility and animosity we were feeling. Ideas were floated back and forth between us many times as to how we should deal with Steven Lee in a manner which would serve to defuse his outbreaks of temper and profanity, but to no avail.

One fine day we had a visit from the Regional District's bylaw enforcement officer, who informed us there had been a complaint of an illegal suite in our home and that it would have to be shut down if it wasn't family living in it! Anyone is allowed two boarders in their home without a license, so the way the Regional District enforced it's bylaw was simply to remove the kitchen stove from the home if the suite wasn't legal.That suite had been in our home for fifteen years, was built to code, but was technically illegal because there were no single family homes on the Westside with legal suite status at that time. Someone simply wanted to make life difficult for us and we suspected instantly who that someone was! We unplugged the stove for some time and Dianne ate with us as she often did anyway. The tension increased between Lee and us as he must have known it would.

Lee started making faces and obscene gestures at Carol and Dianne whenever he could garner their attention! If either of the girls were outside in the yard and he saw them then he would make a sound to attract their attention and then give them a finger, or a hand wave from the nose, that kind of thing! It was so hard to believe at first that they were both kind of shocked by his infantile behavior! This was a grown man, with children of his own, totally unprovoked, behaving in an inexplicable, unbelievable manner! To us his behavior wasn't simply inexplicable but often offensive.While we couldn't understand Lee's behavior at all, we finally understood what the kids had been trying to tell us about this man. We now knew that he had a hate for us and he wanted us to know he was going to make life miserable for us. At this point I thought that we could handle anything he threw at us if we remained calm, didn't react, just tried to peacefully coexist.............. **I was wrong!!**

Our home was the last on the street located on a turn-around. There were only houses on our side of the road as there was an orchard directly across from us that ran the whole block. The Lees lived on one side of us and there was a good sized forest on the other side of us in which all of the neighborhood children played. Many people enjoyed hiking through that forest and you could actually go straight up the heavily treed mountain from our home, right on to Morning Star Bible camp and beyond.Located below us were rows of homes on different roads. The mountain sloped down all the way to the lake and our windows oriented in this direction to take advantage of the gorgeous view of the Okanagan Lake. Our decks at both levels faced the lake as did the Lee family's decks. Their home was built further down the mountain by about sixty feet.

Whenever we used our deck the front corner of the Lee deck was directly in our line of sight and there was Steven Lee just waiting. He would shout profanities, howl like a dog, or simply glare at whoever was on our deck to the point where we would become uncomfortable and go inside. Imagine how you or your guests would feel if someone did this to you in the sanctuary of your own yard, regardless of who was visiting you! It was an intolerable situation, which placed an increasing amount of stress on the whole family!

Carol would be relaxing in her yard, perhaps with Dianne or her parents, maybe visiting or having a coffee or afternoon tea, and out would come Steven Lee for no other reason than to cause an incident. He seemed to take some perverse delight in upsetting people! This psychotic behavior gave him a sense of power and made him feel superior to others! He was had to control every situation, which he did by causing it!

It really didn't seem to matter where we went, Lee could walk around the outskirts of our yard and continue his harassment of different members of our family, whenever he was at home and he happened to feel in the mood..To begin with, aside from the first shouting incident with David, Steven Lee did nothing in front of me. Most of the problems occurred with other members of my family while I was at work, and I never witnessed them taking place, but heard about them from members of our family.I guess I thought that he was an overprotective parent looking after his family the best he knew how. Lee had recently moved to a new neighborhood and I supposed it was natural for him to react this way until he got a feel for the area. I supposed he would settle down especially after he had satisfied himself that there was nothing here that posed any threat to him or his family. The incidents seemed quite innocuous and infrequent at first and I dismissed them from my mind almost as quickly as they were related to me. Lee's brazen actions gradually increased in frequency and intensity over time to the point where I knew that sooner or later I was going to have to deal with him and it wasn't going to be pleasant.

Steven Lee mowed lawns, pruned hedges, and did small construction renovations, and he was always looking for new customers. In reality Lee was getting a feel for the neighborhood, building up a clientele, deciding who he would befriend. He wasn't a stupid person who would bite the hand that fed him. If it was advantageous for him to be nice, he could be very nice and he took his time deciding who he should be nice to.If he looked after your yard presumably you had nothing to worry about, you were okay with Lee. This is why it was so difficult to get an accurate picture of the man from the beginning.

One of his favorite habits was to drive up the road and then deliberately go the wrong way around the turnaround. This put him on the wrong side of the road as he came directly in front of our home. One might suppose this to be a little thing or at worst a bad habit. It gave him a great view of our yard between our cedars, but we had to tell our smaller children to be careful about vehicles driving close to our hedge. It was a mild irritant to us, but one of many with which we learned to cope.

One day I overheard Lee talking to his twelve year old daughter in a manner that absolutely flabbergasted me. He wasn't upset or angry but he was using every foul four lettered word you might expect to hear on a construction site! I couldn't believe my ears, that a father would talk like this in a normal conversation with his young daughter, was mind boggling to me! Shiela Lee was maybe thirteen years old at the time and I felt so sorry for her that it was all I could do to stop myself from openly questioning him about such reprehensible behavior! I know our kids have to grow up and learn to function in this difficult and trying world, but I have always believed they have the right to enjoy their childhood first!

This troubled me deeply then, as it does to this day when I think about it. In a family environment children are normally afforded some protection by their parents from offensive, foul mouthed, crass behavior This was not the case in the Lee family! Call me simple; call me naive; but Steven Lee was the most openly offensive, foul mouthed man in front of his or anyone's children that I have ever met! He never cared what he said in front of anybody's kids especially when he lost his temper! **How can anyone..... especially children.... be expected to respect a man such as this?**

We were reported to the Regional District for our illegal basement suite several more times. One evening I had a 200 foot hose and caddy stolen from under my steps. Very few people knew I even had it let alone where it was stored..... **Lee knew!** I had a new paint job applied to my truck, but a few days later someone ran a key or nail the length of the truck...... I can't prove it was Lee! I cannot prove that a distinctive towel, removed from our outside clothes line was taken by Lee,but in a newspaper photograph for which he posed, there is our towel sitting on his woodpile directly behind him! The towel was distinctive, one of two given to Carol and myself when we left Saskatchewan as a parting gift. Under normal circumstances the towel would have had little significance, but whenever I revisit that picture and see the towel on his woodpile with Lee posing in front of it, I must confess it still bothers me!

Halloween was upon us and as was the Demers custom we had a bonfire where we roasted wieners for hotdogs and followed up with marsh mellows. A sing song and some scary stories would follow as we enjoyed fellowship around the fire. Various friends and neighborhood kids would stop-over to warm up and have a cup of hot chocolate or a coffee as they made their rounds for treats.

As the evening was coming to an end and we finished our cleanup, extinguished our fire and went into the house, a knock came to the door.

I answered the knock and there stood Steven Lee holding the remains of a shattered pumpkin in his hand. He went on to tell me there had been a bang outside and by the time he got there whoever had set the firecrackers in his pumpkin was gone. With that he turned and with as angry a scowl as I've ever seen threw the pumpkin remains as high up over the street as he could! Down it came bursting into a thosand pieces as it contacted the pavement!I told him that all my kids were at home with the family and that I had been present at all times, but that I would check with them and see if they knew anything about it. I told him that I would let him know what I found out. The boys knew who had done the deed and they told me who it was. It had been someone from the school they all attended who had a personal grudge with Troy Lee. No harm had been done aside from a smashed pumpkin and I decided that it wasn't going any further. I told Lee nothing as I knew he would only over react and that as a result no good would come to anyone.

Carol and Dianne used to enjoy going on walks together and even alone or with one of our kids at different times. Lee seemed to always be watching them and sometimes he even got in his vehicle and followed them making sure that they knew that he was following them. It was very unnerving for them and extremely uncomfortable to know he wasn't far behind them. Sometimes he leered or glared at them and other times he would just drive by and shout an insult or swear at them. These actions were witnessed by neighbors on more than one occasion!

My nine year old son Matthew, a quiet little boy who never bothered anyone was sitting on the lawn one day relaxing under a birch tree when Lee pulled up in his vehicle and parked on the wrong side of the street as was his custom. As he got out of his vehicle he sneered at Matthew, " **Hello, you little fag!**" Carol happened to see him talking to our son and as Matthew came into the house she questioned him about what Mr. Lee had said. Matt was reluctant to answer, but when pressed, obediently told his mom what Lee had said to him. There was a tear in his eye as he told his mom that it didn't matter and not to tell dad. When I heard this story I honestly didn't know what to do? I wanted to grab that guy and knock the stuffing out of him at first.... but as the anger subsided, I felt so much sympathy for my little boy, who even at that tender age was smart enough to know that this would only cause more trouble with the **jerk** living next door!

I was told however, and frankly I didn't know what to do about it or just how to handle it? What do you say to a man that talks to an innocent child in this fashion? I instructed the kids to try and avoid Lee, but how were they to avoid him in their own yard.... minding their own business, if he came looking for them? After all he lived next door! It was obvious if Steven Lee wished to provoke an incident with any member of our family it would be impossible to prevent it!

At different times over the years my good wife was called a slut and a bitch by Steven Lee, for having so many children!? It mattered not that the children were neat and tidy, well mannered and considered respectful of neighbors and adults in general. A better mother you wouldn't find anywhere, anytime, any place.

My thoughts were and still are that if a person couldn't get along with Carol and Dianne then they probably couldn't get along with anyone! These were two of the nicest, friendliest women, I have ever known! In my mind I couldn't reconcile why we were having all these problems developing between these two women; these children; and this one man! I had to face the realization that this nut case was deliberately provoking these incidents!

For whatever reason, Lee was determined to make life intolerable for the Demers family. Maybe he wanted us to move, maybe he wanted everyone in the neighborhood to know that he was the boss.... I don't know. Slowly the realizatiion that there would be no peaceful coexistence with Mr. Lee began to force itself into my consciousness..... as much as I tried not to accept it, there would be no appeasing this nut case! What would he do next, I wondered, just what was he capable of? I thought about purchasing some security cameras and mounting them on our home, facing them towards our property line so I could have some concrete evidence of what was going on. Taking this action would no doubt have infuriated Lee, which I was trying to avoid, so I decided against it.

One long weekend a realtor friend and chess partner of mine headed to Vancouver to play chess in the Keres Memorial Chess Tournament. We left on a Friday evening and wouldn't be arriving home until late Monday evening. The next day a co-worker from the telephone company dropped over to have a coffee with Carol. Lee saw the B.C. Tel. van out in front of the house and thinking he could make trouble for me called into the company to report that I was at home when I should be at work!Lee called three times over the next twenty minutes speaking to the same supervisor each time. He was never told that I wasn't working, but only that the supervisor wasn't going to get involved in a dispute between neighbors. He went on to explain that some employees took their vehicles home because of service demands or call outs, or special arrangements made with the company, or when they were working out of their headquarters areas, etc. etc. etc.! To this day Stephen Lee thinks that I was at home when I was being paid to work, even though the company knew I was not shifted, not working, and not even in town!

My immediate supervisor raised the incident with me the following Tuesday morning, when I returned to work, which was the first time I heard about it. Carol had told me about the co-worker stopping to have coffee with her, but the company knew I was off that weekend and really wasn't too interested in finding out which of their employees had stopped at my place for a coffee. Besides they knew who was working that day, he was quite active in the union and the effort required to pursue the matter would not have justified the final outcome. I was advised to watch out for this neighbor however as he was going to be trouble, **as if I didn't know!**

Lee's father passed away and he went to the lower mainland to settle business affairs. As he was going to be away for approximately ten days we thought we would plant some small cedars between our property lines just on the other side of our children's jungle gym set. We purposely stayed within the property line so as to avoid any conflict. In all there were a total of ten trees planted which would provide some privacy as they grew and a nice looking buffer between the Lee yard and our children's jungle gym.

I remember the evening that Steven Lee arrived home. It was a beautiful evening sun still shining about 6:45P. M. when he pulled up and parked on the wrong side of the road. Leaping out of his truck he eyeballed the trees as he sighted down the property line. He had obviously been kept well informed of what was going on by his wife and he was loaded for bear!I happened to be reading a chess book at the desk in our kitchen and was directly in front of the window and clearly visible to Lee as he started hollering at me and signaling me to come out. While I couldn't make out what he was saying there was no mistaking from his body language that it wasn't going to be a pleasant experience! The guy had bragged that he was a martial arts expert and that his hands were registered with the police which didn't fill me with confidence.

Out I went in my house slippers towards our property lines where Lee was standing waving his arms and directing a barrage of curse words towards me! I really don't have to tell you what kind of a f—ing ass——I was I'm sure! We both started swinging at each other and Lee said I took the first swing. I'll accept that, if it means anything. He wasn't inviting me out for a barbeque!Sometimes frustration will out and the months of putting up with the antics of this guy finally surfaced! Before I knew what was happening Lee's Boxer was on me and out his wife came carrying a stick about five feet long, hollering for us to stop. Steven went down to his yard walked over to our newly planted trees then looked up at me and in a threatening manner scowled, " **Don't think this is over yet!**" I replied, **"If it's not over get back up here and let's finish it!"**

Two police cars came roaring up the street toward us as Lee's wife had called them before coming out. As the constables approached us I watched Mr. Steven Lee's personality change instantly from tiger to pussycat as he quietly told his wife, " I've got to talk to the officers and he turned into the sweetest nicest guy I've **never** seen! I watched and listened as Mr. **Nice Guy** sweet talked the officers about how it was just a problem with neighborhood kids. He was downplaying the significance of this whole affair; trivializing the incident and what had led up to it by blaming it all on my kids! He conned those policemen right there in front of us and I don't blame them one bit for believing him. Lee was smooth and polished and so cool in contrast to me; flushed, panting heavily from the wild swinging and so frustrated and angry over what had been going on for so long, I was anything but cool!

Right there and then, Steven Lee taught me a lesson I'll never forget! This guy had been through these affairs with the police before and he knew exactly what he was doing and how to handle this situation! When the officers thought they had heard enough and that the situation was under control they more or less left us with the thought that they couldn't be responding to incidents such as this! They continued that one of us should consider moving to which I responded it wasn't going to be us, and away they went.

The next day while at work I noticed that Lee's vehicle was parked at the local surveyor's office, no doubt checking on what it would cost to have his boundary lines between our two homes checked! What I found so hard to understand was that the small cedars I had planted between our properties actually improved the looks and privacy for both properties! The trees would eventually screen out the view of our little girls jungle gym set which most people would have considered a mutual benefit.The trees were definitely inside our property line and I didn't require any permission to plant them anyway! Why did they make him so angry? I'll never be able to figure the answer to that question out! Lee was supposed to be a landscaper, but for the rest of his time there he did everything in his power to kill those trees.

One of his tricks was to use his weed wacker under the pretence of trimming weeds and then proceed to strip the bottom six inches of bark off our newly planted trees. When I noticed this I took the first opportunity at night and placed rocks around the base of the cedars. These carefully placed rocks disappeared very quickly even though they were on our property. Finally one night I took the time to wire some metal flashing around the base of the cedars. At this point Lee resigned himself to the fact that aside from poisoning or cutting them down, the trees were there to stay!

I had decided to see a lawyer and try to get some advice on what to do about this situation. I went to get my will drawn up at Lyle Brown's Law office in Westbank, and had a thorough conversation with him about what had been going on since Lee had moved to our neighborhood! We discussed restraining orders; their effect; and their enforcement. The conclusion we reached was that we could spend an easy ten thousand dollars and in the final analysis still be sharing the same property line with Lee anyway.Lyle suggested that we give a great deal of thought to moving! At that point I just couldn't bring myself to seriously consider leaving our home! We had so many fond memories there of our children and my parents over the last fourteen years, that I simply thought there had to be another solution! It was out of the question that we were going to leave that home!

News of the confrontation between Lee and myself spread over the neighborhood like wildfire. Now the animosity between us was no longer a secret. It became the topic of conversation among the neighbors as the news spread. Certainly people chose to believe what they wanted and that was their right. I always felt that sooner or later the truth would emerge anyway. The Demers family had lived here for fifteen years and tried to be good members of our community. Our kids had paper routes in the neighbourhood, attended school and church there and we had never had a problem with any of our neighbours before.

Three houses down the road from us lived Don and Judy Harvey and their three children, Christie, Jarret, and Jenna. Judy's sister lived in a basement suite in their home with her two kids, one of which chummed around with our boy Mark. His name was Jeff Severson and he and Mark were great friends. The two boys (both thirteen) used to visit back and forth between our homes as most friends do.Early one evening they were walking towards the Harvey home as Lee was driving up the road towards his place. The two boys were laughing and talking as they walked and Lee as he drove by got the idea that they were laughing and joking at or about him! Lee circled his vehicle around at the turnaround and came back down the road and pulled up beside the two boys who by this time were almost to the Harvey home. Here he began to challenge the boys about laughing and joking at him. He didn't like the response he got and began to swear at the boys shouting something about them not respecting him.

Don Harvey was working out in his yard, heard the disturbance and walked up to the road to see what was going on. When he saw and heard his nephew and Mark being sworn at he immediately walked over to Lee and asked him to explain his actions. Lee turned on Don and shouted that these boys didn't have any respect for him and Lee was going to kick their heads up their asses if they didn't smarten up and give him some respect!Don replied that respect was something that should be mutual and that judging by his actions Lee didn't respect the rights of others so why should he expect any in return? Lee had a short fuse and challenged Don to a fight right there and then. Don remained calm, declined to fight, preferring to try and find an amiable way to solve this incident. He managed to calm Lee down and get him to understand that he couldn't go around calling the neighborhood kids names and swearing at them whenever he felt like it!

Their conversation lasted for about twenty minutes when they finally headed towards their respective homes. Lee seemed satisfied for the time being that Jeff and Mark were going to be wary as he had served notice on them to watch the way they acted. He had stood toe to toe with Don Harvey and let him know that he was ready to fight anytime!Don Harvey stood about six feet two inches tall and was well muscled. I don't think he was afraid to fight Lee at anytime, but he was a quiet Christian man, just trying to be a good neighbor by his example. He was an intelligent cool headed man who desired peaceful coexistence in our neighborhood. I didn't know the Harvey's having only spoken briefly to them the odd time I had seem them passing our home as they went walking through the forest.

Mark told us the whole story when he got home. While I empathized with Don, I was relieved that someone else had finally had a similar experience to ours with Lee. Maybe an ally was just what the Demers family needed. Someone else in the neighborhood would finally understand how difficult this new neighbor was proving to be to get along with! A few days after his incident with Lee, Don was walking by our home and stopped to talk with me about what had happened.

We spent a good deal of time going over much of what had transpired between each member of our families and Mr. Steven Lee's part in each confrontation. By the end of our conversation we were pretty much in agreement that we had a king size problem in our neighborhood. However Don and I really didn't know each other and at this point no definite plans as to how to proceed were made. I really felt a faint glimmer of hope that if enough people in the neighborhood came to understand the situation that some pressure could be brought to bear on Steven Lee by them and perhaps he would settle down. At any rate it sure wouldn't hurt to have some allies in this situation if only to distract Lee's attention from being focused exclusively on the Demers family.

One day Lee stopped my son David as he was walking home. **"Hey I've got a message for your old man. Tell him I'm going to off him and blow his f—ing house up!"** I got the message loud and clear and even though I really didn't believe it I couldn't forget it either. Something like that stays with you, plays over and over in your mind whether you're sleeping or awake, you cannot will yourself to forget it! Again I found myself churning these remarks over and over in my mind, as the thought continued to haunt me...... just how far would this guy go?!

Matthew and Phillip had paper routes which they inherited from their brothers and sisters before them. The paper was dropped off in three large bundles in front of the house during the night in preparation for delivery the next day. At least once a week one of the bundles began disappearing as if the boys had been shorted. We would have to call the company who very soon got fed up with having to get another driver to deliver us more papers before the boys could do their deliveries! We requested the papers be left inside our storage shed when we finally figured out what was causing the trouble. Steven Lee was removed from our list of people to deliver to as he already had way more copies than he could read anyway! Of course he raised hell with the newspaper, but we were prepared to let them find someone else to do the routes which our kids had faithfully delivered for a number of years.

One night as we were readying ourselves for bed Carol called me to the kitchen. She had turned off the lights and gone back to the kitchen for a glass of water. As she was having a drink she was looking out the window and noticed something crawling down the property line between our place and Lee's.

There was our neighbor crawling on hands and knees along the property line in the dark! We watched for awhile in disbelief, but as we couldn't see clearly what he was doing , we lost interest and went to bed. Several days later we began to notice that a couple of our sprinklers weren't functioning properly and we realized what he had been up to a few nights before. He still wanted to kill those newly planted trees of ours.

On another occasion Carol noticed Steven Lee pull out of his yard very late at night. About forty minutes later back he came with a full load of lumber. We wondered where one goes for lumber at midnight as the only place we could think of was " Gorman's Lumbar Mill"? Maybe the lumber came from a friend who didn't get off work until after midnight and wanted Steven to come and pick it up right away. We don't know for sure, but after watching this guy for a time we became very suspicious of everything he did! Who could you tell and what could you prove, believe me it became a maddening preoccupation with me!

One beautiful July morning as we were enjoying a coffee a knock came to the door. Carol opened the door to face an R.C.M.P. constable who introduced himself as constable Tysec called to investigate a broken window next door at the Lee residence. Apparently Lee had a broken window in his basement which he believed our son David had caused! When constable Tysec arrived to investigate Steven Lee was not at home so in order to save time the constable had come over to interview David while he waited for Lee to come home. After talking to our son, the constable asked us what had been going on from our point of view so we gave him our side of the story. We laid the history of the conflict out for him and asked for his recommendations as to what we could do to resolve our problems. Constable Tysec replied that in many instances such as this that the law was reactive rather than proactive. A sad fact of life is that often nothing is done to prevent situations such as this from arising, but after the law is broken the police really have to get involved!

I was so frustrated by this time as I felt that we were at our wits end in trying to deal with this guy next door! I made it clear that Lee made his own rules and was careful there were never any witnesses around when he knowingly broke the law! The constable completed his interview, excused himself, and headed over to the Lee house to talk to Mr.

Lee. Constable Tysec spent about half an hour going over the accusations a very angry Steven Lee was making against my son David, before returning to our home to talk to us again. He began by telling us that he had decided after listening to Lee that there was absolutely no evidence to support Lee's allegations against David and that no charges would be forthcoming!

Constable Tysec went on to state that Steven Lee was in a highly agitated state, that he had demanded the officer's badge number and threatened that if no action was taken in this matter that he would take matters into his own hands! The constable replied that if Lee did that then the law would deal with him! Lee finally asked the police officer whom he had called, to leave his property. We were very relieved to hear that the allegations were in fact found to be groundless and thanked the officer as he prepared to leave. We were shocked however when Constable Tysec said that with Lee being as upset as he was perhaps we should keep a low profile around our home until he had some time to cool off! I couldn't believe that we were getting a warning to kind of lay low so as not to rile Lee anymore! In effect we now felt like prisoners in our own home!

In reality we had been warned that Lee had openly threatened to take matters into his own hands. Tysec knew that Lee was a hothead when he got into his squad car and drove off, but so far there was little he could do. Meanwhile there wasn't much we could do but wait for whatever came next! Our laws are more reactive than proactive in this country.

After two years of living next to this guy and getting a few more pieces of advice from people we valued, a decision was made to put our home up for sale! When your peace of mind and joy of living goes out of each day, you begin to think the unthinkable. As much as we loved our home we just had to put an end to this nightmare! I listed the property with a realtor friend, John Neufeld, in September of 1994.

The fellows at work felt that I was giving in, and selling the house for all the wrong reasons. I was being bullied into moving; into leaving a home we loved rather than standing up to the guy. The worst of it was that I agreed with them! They were right; we were being pushed out of a place that nobody in our family wanted to leave!

No sooner did the sign go up on the property then Lee openly bragged to Don Harvey that the Demers family could run, but they couldn't hide! Don replied that Lee should be happy to see us leave the neighborhood and inquired why he didn't seem to be? Lee replied, " **I've got my reasons**"!? The really scary thing to me was that only Lee knew what those reasons were and he was never able to clearly define to anyone so far as we know what those reasons were or why he held them? All we were ever able to understand is that he resented our whole family with a deep seated hatred bordering on insanity!

Lee scared the hell out of me because his behavior was so unpredictable. He had a lot of guns(nine) and used to take his son up in the bush to shoot at times. Other times he went by himself, up past our home marching as a soldier where he would stop do a little pirouette and give an improvised gun drill for my wife and kids to watch! He would actually point the gun and sight down the barrel in different directions as he aimed the weapon at imaginary targets! Then after he was sure they had seen him he would continue on his way, smirking with satisfaction!What reason could a person have for such behavior? He once bragged openly to one of our neighbors that he could pick one of the Demers kids off from his doorstep without anyone ever knowing! **Was that the behavior of a normal man? Was he really thinking he could shoot one of our kids!?!**

These veiled threats continued coming to us from different people who had spoken to Lee on various occasions. In many instances they were as shocked as we were and advised us to alert the authorities. We checked with acquaintances on the police force who knew how the law works and the best advice we could get was to move! Believe me when I say that while we loved our home, gradually the unthinkable was becoming thinkable!

In many cases in Canada the law is reactive not proactive and some law must be broken before the authorities will act! Threats are difficult to prove, are expensive to deal with through the courts, and often wind up being thrown out leaving the plaintiff with nothing but a huge bill to pay. Does the end result justify all the effort and costs that a litigant incurs trying to hold someone accountable for threats through the court system? Most people never have to concern themselves with questions such as these, because for the most part neighbours are friendly and respectful of their neighbours property and rights. Up until this time that had always been our experience anyway.

The Harvey family was added to Lee's list enemies and he began to hassle them whenever the opportunity presented itself. If he happened to see Judy or Don, Lee would make some rude gesture or holler some insult or maybe just give them that special glare of his. Whatever Lee chose to do was guaranteed to make his victim feel very uncomfortable at the time. He never failed to provoke some kind of unpleasant incident which he could use to gain control over people. It seemed to be his only reason for living so far as we could tell. Lee's actions were extremely upsetting to people because of their shock value. When a woman encounters a man who begins by calling her a slut in a very loud threatening manner, the initial reaction is one of disbelief and shock! While the victim is still trying to make sense of what has just happened Lee would then continue his verbal assault in conjunction with extremely aggressive body language which scared the daylights out of them!

He really seemed to get a perverse sense of pleasure out of creating situations at every opportunity which put him in control. The Harvey's were now experiencing some of what the Demers family was going through and just like us, wondered what was wrong with this guy!

Lee got a job painting a neighbor's house, located directly below us. The owner, Mrs. Fox, was quite deaf and lived alone since her husband had been placed in a senior's home. Lee mowed her lawn and now he had the job of painting her house.When he wanted to attract Carol's attention he would just turn his radio way up. When Carol would go to see what the disturbance was about Lee would be standing on top of the Fox's roof making faces at her. He was able to look straight in our living room window while standing on that roof, so Carol kept her drapes closed, whenever he was working on the Fox house.

Fall came, and while our home was for sale, we found a place we liked with a lovely suite in it, and made an offer subject to financing. As sad as I was at having to leave our home, I was looking forward to getting away from Lee and all the trouble. Although it was very reasonably priced we never got an offer on our home, perhaps it was just a lull in the market, or maybe bad news travels fast; I really don't know for certain. At any rate our house just didn't sell at that time and I had very mixed emotions about that.

We had tolerated this guy for about two and a half years and were at our wits end. The constant stress of dealing with Lee was making me ill. There was a war being waged against my family by this psychopath for a long time and I seemed powerless to stop it! When I decided to sell and move, Lee saw it as a victory for him! When our home didn't sell I really began to panic. In my mind I felt trapped, there seemed to be no escape from this nut case no matter what I tried!

At the end of each working day I dreaded the thoughts of going home to hear what Steven Lee had done to some member of our family. Lee knew the way to get to me was through my family and anything he could do to bother them had a direct effect on me.

There seemed to be something that had happened every day to disturb someone in our family. Whether Lee was cutting through our yard to get to Mrs. Fox's house or his dog was crapping in our yard, just anything to let us know he was on us day in, day out! Everybody felt like prisoners in our home. Carol often asked me what I was going to do about Lee? Lee had become my number one problem in life!At work or play, at home or away, awake or asleep, every moment of my life, Steven Lee was there! What would he do next? Maybe I was becoming paranoid; were my fears real or imagined; I didn't know what this man was capable of! I had no idea of his background or history, whether he had a criminal record or not, I just didn't know!

I knew he wasn't normal because as I mentioned, normal men don't bully women and children; don't make the type of threats designed to scare women and kids such as his actions with his gun drills or threats that he could pick off my kids from his doorstep and no one would ever know! Normal men don't threaten to blow up your home at night!Perhaps my mind was playing tricks on me; thinking the unthinkable;

but those thoughts had in most cases been placed there by Steven Lee's threats! He was the one responsible for making me think that my home might burn down some night! Steven Lee once told Carol, "You are going to be sorry you ever lived next to me!" he also said "You have no idea what I'm capable of!"

Those remarks were made to Carol, in the presence of Mrs. Dianne Roth during an afternoon tea. These were what I refer to as implied or veiled threats designed to worry a person, but too vague for the law to act on.

I can only say as winter came that I felt deeply depressed at not being able to solve the problem of Steven Lee. While

I wasn't really conscious of changes in my behavior, other family members and friends began to notice, although they said little to me. I was withdrawn much of the time, becoming a brooding person, almost reclusive in my home, daydreaming to the point I often didn't seem to hear what other's said to me.Our home didn't sell and we were trapped in a situation with a psychopath, waiting for whatever he had in store for us! Everything we had tried had failed and Lee had become more brazen in his actions. By this time I was wound up tighter than a coiled spring, ready to explode! Things were much worse for me when I was at home on days off, as I was there to see what happened and forced to deal with it immediately! I began to feel like a prisoner in my own home, not wanting to go outside knowing that a confrontation with Lee was inevitable!

The Christmas holidays were upon us, normally a time of great joy for our family. The wonderful fellowship that a large family shared at this time of year made this special time even more precious to us! There was a type of foreboding upon us this year though, as we tried to get into the Christmas spirit, but carried the uneasy feeling that an incident with Steven Lee was always just around the corner. Christmas came and went rather uneventfully and New Years Eve was here. Steven Lee and a friend, had apparently received permission from someone to take down a huge coniferous tree on some private property about two hundred feet straight up the mountain from our home. This they chose to begin at midnight on New Years Eve!

They had a fire going up there and were drinking as they set about felling the huge tree and then bucking up the wood. By the sounds coming from up the mountain that they were going to make a real party of it! It really didn't concern us much and was only mildly interesting to us, simply because Lee was never up to any good so far as we were concerned. As I said before, you never really knew what the guy was going to do next, but he was usually up to no good.New Years Day passed with Lee and Gibbs continuing to cut and haul their wood down the mountain, past our home and on to their respective houses. The second day of January dawned with them finishing up the job they had begun and after many trips back and forth past our home nary an incident occurred.

My son Mark and I were enjoying the " World Junior Hockey Championships" on television and were some hyped when Canada won the gold medal! We were cheering the team on as if we were at the game ourselves, enjoying Canada's victory celebrations! I was on my way to the kitchen when I overheard Dianne asking Carol what had just happened. Carol replied that as she was preparing supper at the sink Lee had given her the finger and hollered something at her which she couldn't make out, but by his gestures didn't appear to be very nice!

In and of itself this was only a small insignificant incident, maybe it was the last straw, but something simply snapped in my mind! I opened the hall closet door in front of me and put my coffee cup down, grabbed my shotgun, some shells, a jacket, my boots and headed back down the hall and out the door! I put the boots on threw some shells in the gun and headed up the mountain to confront Lee! He was coming down the mountain with a wheelbarrow full of wood almost down to the road in front of my home when I met him. As soon as he saw me with the gun he hollered " You're in trouble now" and I raised the gun and fired. **Bang!** The gun discharged with a boom, but nothing happened!?! Lee was still standing there directly in front of me, eyes open wide, staring in disbelief! Had I missed; with a shotgun; at this range?! What had just happened? What now?

My mind was racing, my heart pumping so fast I thought it was going to burst; as we faced each other in shock and disbelief as time seemed to stop .... Lee walked towards me as I stood between him and his home. He walked right up to me and I shoved that shotgun right in his mouth! I never wanted to kill anyone in my life, but right at that moment, that thought reverberated through my mind as we faced each other!.......with every ounce of my being I wanted to squeeze that trigger again...... to eliminate this problem forever!My brain was trying frantically to process all the information being sent it, but the messages were mixed....... unclear...... What was happening? My mind couldn't quite process what was happening ..... The gun had fired but Lee was still standing ????? Had I missed ???? I couldn't have missed ..... if I had, did I fire a warning???? I didn't want it to come to this ...... this .... why had he pushed me to this???? it was all so unreal..... A living nightmare!

But here he was.... standing right in front of me and my twelve gage shotgun was stuck in his mouth .... for what seemed an eternity we stood not knowing what to do! I know all I ever wanted was for this guy to leave my family alone, that was my whole reason for being here now!!! I had him completely at my mercy and should have been able to get him to say or do anything I wanted; **I had Lee right where I wanted him! I said nothing ...... Lee said nothing.....** that's the only time I saw him absolutely speechless!!! So many thoughts raced through my mind as we stood there, but gradually it became clear, (maybe to both of us) that I couldn't pull that trigger again.... I knew in my heart if I squeezed that trigger the blast would have taken his head clear off ! Lee must have known that as well with all the guns he had; so he stood there.... quiet and still as we faced each other..... not knowing what to do???

Gradually Lee sensed that I wasn't going to shoot and he pushed the gun barrel to the side of his head and started to moan! The moan became a howl and he started running and as he ran I aimed the gun at him, hesitated, until he was about sixty feet away and....**Bang.....**shot him right in the rear! He just kept going, without looking back and I took off after him. When Lee got down to his house he stopped..... turned around and faced me again..... It was the most bizarre unreal experience I have ever had! It was as if I was watching a horrible movie in which I seemed powerless to stop what was happening! As Lee stood in front of his house looking at me, I fired again, **Bang.....** and he turned and disappeared into his house!

I had fired this twelve gauge pump action shotgun three times directly at this individual with apparently no effect whatsoever?! This was totally unreal, bizarre, unbelievable, and incomprehensible to me at that time! My mind couldn't process the information properly!

I ran back to my yard, grabbed my jacket and some more shells and headed up the mountain into the forest. The whole shooting incident had taken approximately three minutes from start to finish **although it seemed much longer!** Darkness was falling fast as I entered the forest shaking and in a daze. At this point not a single person in my family had any knowledge of what had just happened! Everyone was inside the house night was falling and the curtains had all been closed as the interior lights were turned on. Television was on and the kids were playing in their rooms while Carol and Dianne were visiting and preparing supper in the kitchen.~

Chapter Four

Greener Pastures

—ᴥ—

Moving to Prince Albert, Saskatchewan, a small city of thirty thousand, was a real change from Meadow Lake, a small town of two thousand. Grade six saw me at St.Mark's Separate School which was a Catholic school. My friend Larry McDougald, had introduced me to the Maneagre family which was the reason I eventually got hired to work as a guide up at Waskesiu. Larry and I remained friends throughout our school years and had some great times growing up.We shared an interest in horses and used to compete in rodeos together. Bareback Bronc riding, Cow riding, Wild Horse racing and Cow milking were our specialty events. Larry always had horses and used to invite me out often to ride with him.

Larrys' dad, Ted, was an extremely charismatic individual whom you liked immediately, yet were a little afraid of as soon as you met him! He was a big man, an auctioneer by trade, with a booming voice. He was a real gambler that you soon learned not to shoot your mouth off in front of ! If he heard you say something that he thought was out of line, or perhaps was an exaggeration, he would call you on it "to put up or shut up"! A person might find themselves having to prove what came out of their mouth's was in fact true.Ted McDougald owned land just north of town which bordered on the "Red River Park". The "Red River" ran right through his property. Right at the bottom was a natural basin where the river snaked around it. You could look down on this location from the higher mesa on which Ted had built their home. The slope down to the river basin was heavily grassed and formed a natural seating area for a sizeable crowd. With it's stands of Ponderosa Pine and Poplar and the little river winding through it, this was a beautiful place to host an outdoor event. There Ted built a race track, a barn, an outdoor arena and chutes for bucking stock, and brought the first rodeo to Prince Albert, Saskatchewan!

Ted was a visionary, who with the right help, could have been a very great man! He had served with the army in the European Theatre and brought a wife back from Holland. He was the Reeve of his rural municipality and later became the local Liberal candidate for government. The Western Producer, did at least one article on his successful launch of "Rodeo" in Prince Albert. He was also a brooding man, and even though he had a hearty laugh and an infectious sense of humor, I saw him lose his temper once and it scared the daylights out of me!

I was invited on a picnic with the McDougald family, consisting of Larry, Teddy, Spenser and their parents. We kids were playing by the lake when, for what reason I don't know, Ted just grabbed Mrs. McDougald by the hair and hauled her out into the water and submerged her! I was dumbfounded! We watched in silence until the ordeal ended and never talked about it again, but the picture of Mrs. McDougald being dragged out into the lake is indelibly engraved on my mind! Only once did I get a glimpse of the rage simmering just below this complex man's charismatic exterior..... but it was an ominous sign of things to come.

Larry and I, entered the wild cow riding in P.A.'s first rodeo, where I got thrown into a rain soaked arena and the cow stepped right on my family jewels! I honestly thought I was done for as I was carried out behind the chutes and laid on the ground! My pants were opened and I was left there to die! Strangely everyone just seemed to ignore me after that, but I didn't really care as I lay there , thinking that I was never going to fulfill my destiny! I didn't die, but I did have the biggest black and blue testicles you ever saw, for a week! Eventually everything returned to normal and my fear that I would never produce offspring later proved to be groundless as well!

The promise made to myself, never to ride bucking stock again was soon forgotten, and in P.A.'s second rodeo held in September 1963, I won first prize day money in the men's bareback riding! That was all it took to get me hooked on rodeo.... One small win, and I thought I was on my way to becoming a champion rodeo cowboy. Larry and I rodeoed in P.A., Meadow Lake, Battleford, and also competed in a little britches rodeo in High River, Alberta.

We continued to rodeo for two seasons, then gave it up. Larry and I knew very quickly that we weren't cut out to be successful rodeo stars. Most of the time, we were a little scared of getting hurt, although we never admitted it to one another. We saw some cowboys get badly injured and you begin to think that it's only a matter of time before your turn comes along. Barely having enough money to pay our entry fees, nothing to eat, sleeping in some cowboy's horse trailer, hitchhiking from one rodeo to another or sleeping in the ditch if we didn't get a ride before dark, were all factors which led us to search for fame and fortune elsewhere! What's the saying, "For every one who makes it, there's a thousand that don't"!

After high school Larry married his high school sweetheart, Donna. **Not long afterwards Ted Mc Dougald, shot**

his wife and her girlfriend to death, then killed himself!
Only God knows for certain why these things happen.
Larry and I have visited perhaps ten times since this terrible
tragedy, but we have never spoken a word about it to each
other! It happened and neither of us could change it after the
fact so maybe it was just better left alone and untouched, I
don't know.

During grade eleven I was asked by Mrs. Robinson, (
pseudonym) a mother of four, if I could break one of her
children's horses of a habit it had of rearing up whenever
they were riding it away from their barn? I agreed to try and
spent about a month working with the animal in my spare
time. A rodeo was to be held in " Little Red River Park" in
P.A. and Mrs. Robinson thought if she rode her mare and I
rode the problem horse to the rodeo grounds, it would be
an excellent opportunity to assess how her children's horse
was progressing. The ride was a good ten miles from the
Robinson's farm to" Red River Park", and would take us
approximately four hours.

The ride was going well, the horses were behaving and
we were ahead of schedule. About two miles from the rodeo
grounds in the middle of the forest Mrs. Robinson asked, "
Darwin, do you want to f—k"? I was so flabbergasted I almost
fell off my horse! The question came out of nowhere and I
was taken so completely off guard I just didn't know what to
say!In as manly a voice as I could muster, I stammered that
it was getting late and her family would be wondering where
we were. In reality, I was petrified, and I hoped she would
accept my feeble excuse." Are you sure?', she asked again.
"God help me", I prayed silently, Maybe I figured it wasn't
fair to her husband who was recuperating from two broken
legs? Believe me I knew it was wrong to even consider it,
but in my defense may I say I was young and simply not
prepared for anything like this! I have thought about this
incident several times throughout my life and while I could

offer a few reasons why this happened to me, I'll never really know for certain.... but.... **"Here's to you Mrs. Robinson, Jesus loves you more than you will know"!**

Warne Soyland, moved into my neighborhood during the 62-63 school year, and while he was a year ahead of me we got to be good friends. He topped six feet, had blonde hair and blue eyes, and was a great horseman. Maybe it was our spirit of adventure, or our restless natures, or perhaps a need to hurry up and get on with life, I can't say for certain, but we started talking about how great it would be to live down in Arizona, on a ranch, where you could cowboy all year long without the discomfort of winter. We began making plans to go there by selling most of our possessions to raise the necessary capital required for food and gas to get there.Our plans were to leave just prior to school Christmas break. We would borrow dad's car as he had the plumbing truck and could get by without it until we had the money to pay for it! I would need to get the vehicle registration out of his wallet the evening we left!

Everything readied, at 9:pm that evening it was extremely cold,

(- 60 degrees below Fahrenheit), and even though our vehicles were plugged in dad asked me to start them up and let the engines run for fifteen minutes so they would be sure to start the next day. This I did, rather smugly as it fit right in with my plans.Believe it or not, when I quietly stole out of the house at midnight, and attempted to start the car it wouldn't go! That will give you an idea just how cold it was! When Warne finally got outside I was very, very, cold, but we slipped the car (a 6 cylinder standard shift) into neutral pushed it by hand out to the back lane, then down a short hill, dropped the clutch ... and it started. We were off on our adventure!

We hit the Montana- Saskatchewan border straight south of Regina on Hwy.6 an hour before it opened. I think we crossed the border at 8:am, just around the time that dad discovered his car and his son were missing. Warne and I made good time and within several days we crossed the Utah-Arizona border and stopped to remove our long underwear. You really don't require long underwear at temperatures above 50 degrees! What an adventure we thought we were having as we neared our destination. Soon we could look for a dude ranch to work on!

The Highway Patrolman stopped us in the Kanab Forest area, just thirty-nine miles from the Grand Canyon! He was suspicious when He passed us, going in the opposite direction and thought I was very young to be driving way down there. A few minutes later, he was following right behind us. After pulling us over, I produced the proper papers with the story we were going to visit my uncle in Texas for Christmas. Still skeptical, the officer suggested we turn around and drive back to a gas station about 19 miles, and there he could make a long distance call to my parents, and if they confirmed my story, he would give us a written pass giving us clear sailing for the remainder of the trip.

When we arrived at the gas station, the officer appeared to be having second thoughts as we talked. When he again suggested he should call from the pay phone, I said that we were fine with that, but would he pay for the long distance call, as we had a difficult time in talking my father into this trip in the first place? Reluctantly he agreed, stepped into the telephone booth and attempted to call my dad in Prince Albert, Saskatchewan. After talking to my father and being instructed to teach us a lesson, We were taken back to a little town by the name of, Fredonia, Arizona, (located just 19 miles from the Utah border), and turned over to the local sheriff! He locked me in the cell of the small jail, where I spent the night locked up with a Navaho Indian,(sleeping it off) and I was so scared I never slept a wink all night! Warne really hadn't broken any laws so the sheriff basically let him sleep in the library, which shared the same building, until the next night when he cleared the Navaho out and Warne and I bunked in a jail cell together.

Every morning the sheriff, dressed in cowboy hat, boots, western star on his chest, and open holstered gun on his hip, would come in and make a joke about us still being there. He would then give us some of our own money(which he had previously confiscated) open the cell door and allow us to go across the street to the restaurant for breakfast! The first day he actually took us over and had a coffee with us. I think we were pretty lucky to have been apprehended where we were, and interned in such a small town as Fredonia! We were informed by the sheriff that dad was coming down to get his car, but we were not at all certain what lay in store for us.

While we waited for dad to make his way to Arizona on the bus, we passed the time reading westerns by authors such as Zane Grey, located on the very area in which we were now interned. There was no shortage of reading material as the other half of the jail building in this small town was the public library! It was a dual purpose structure, and the local boy scouts even had some meetings there while Warne and I were guests!The sheriff took us on patrol one evening in his police car, where he met with another patrolman from Utah at the border. The sheriff was a friendly man and he explained that he had been elected to the office for a four year period. I think he owned a small trucking company before becoming sheriff. He had such a Southern drawl as did most people in Fredonia, that we found it difficult at times to understand we were all speaking English!

Dad finally arrived and after a short talk with the sheriff, took Warne and I to the restaurant for breakfast, where we quickly decided we would like to go home! I must say that my father took everything very well and was an especially good sport about what we had done!(he did make us pay for the gas and meals though). I think he really enjoyed our little holiday as well! The trip home was much more enjoyable than it had been going to Arizona, as we were relaxed and no longer nervous about being caught. We shopped all the way home and everyone who got a present from us that year knew it was, " made with Pride in the U.S.A." and of course that we had picked it up in person, on location! It was my first trip south of the 49th Parallel, to the states of Montana, Dakota, Wyoming, Utah, Arizona, and Idaho.My mother was relieved and happy, to have us home safe and sound. Warne's dad and foster mother seemed ambivalent, which may explain why he went in the first place. The two of us returned to Riverside High, with stories to tell willing ears about our pre-Christmas holiday!

I met Carol Fusick in grade ten and was attracted to her immediately. Unfortunately the attraction wasn't mutual, but I persisted and eventually we began to date in grade eleven. Neither Carol nor I ever dreamed that our relationship would become a lifelong marriage of over forty years and be blessed with eight children, but I think God knew it all along! After high school we went our separate ways for a few years, but Carol said a prayer which seemed to tie us inextricably together in spite of the distance between us and the time we were apart.

The Prayer

Heavenly Father up above, Please protect the boy I love,

Keep him safe and keep him sound, No matter where or when he's found,

Help him to know help him to see, That I love him let him love me,

And then Lord help me to be the kind of girl he expects of me,

Keep us now keep us forever, Keep us close and always together,
Grant oh Lord to be content, I thank the Lord for the boy God sent.

Amen

High school days should be fun days and mine were just that, due largely to the fact I played guitar. There were thousands of bands across the country, making music and I played with several during my high school years. At last count the number of musicians I played with was seventeen. Eventually I got the opportunity to play bass in the best rock band in Prince Albert, the "Starfires." We played every hall in P.A. over the next two years. Every talent show and high school wanted us for their dances. Bookings came from out of town as well which kept us busy practicing during the week and playing on the weekends. We did the local television station's "Four O'Clock Hop" show several times, and had a ball doing it all! Sure it was only on a small scale, but even the biggest rock bands started the same way! (Ask the Guess Who). The big difference between us and the professionals was simply that they had much more talent!

The number two band in town was comprised of students who attended P.A.C.I.(Prince Albert Collegiate). Jerry Allbright, the lead guitarist, went on to become a prominent lawyer in Saskatchewan. One of Jerry's most famous cases was his defense of Collin Thatcher (son of premier Ross Thatcher) who was found guilty of murdering his wife! Collin Thatcher was recently granted full parole after serving twenty two years in a federal penitentiary. I've heard that Jerry went on to become a judge in Saskatchewan, quite an accomplishment for which his family is no doubt proud!

One Sunday afternoon I called at Carol's home to take her out for a soda. As she answered the door, she smiled and invited me in for a moment saying she wanted to introduce me to someone. Thinking she had relatives visiting I followed her into the living room to be introduced. There in her parents living room, as God is my witness, **sat the Prime Minister of Canada, Mr. John George Diefenbaker with his wife Olive!** For the first time in my life, I was tongue tied, all I could manage was some goofy remark about the weather, as Mr.Diefenbaker stood to shake my hand! Unknown to me, Carol's family attended the same small Baptist church as the Diefenbakers, and Mrs. Fusick was Olive's, seamstress. I was so completely taken by surprise, at how nonchalant everyone was at entertaining the Prime Minister and his wife for lunch!

Two weeks before final grade twelve exams it became apparent to me that I wasn't going to make the grade. I talked to our drummer Dave and we decided to take off for British Columbia to seek our fame and fortune. Good-bye Saskatchewan hello British Columbia.We headed to Prince George, B.C. which was about 1200 miles away. We chose P.G. after reading an article which featured the huge building boom going on there. New pulp mills were under construction there and the article reported plenty of opportunity for anyone who wanted a job. We found the article to be an accurate report on the opportunities for employment as we both landed jobs our first day in Prince George. Dave got a job at a sawmill and that afternoon I managed to get hired by British Columbia Telephone Company! I didn't know it then but that job became a career lasting almost forty years! I can only say that the Lord provided that job for me! ~

Chapter Five
New Realities

—∿—

One of the new facts of life I had to adjust to while being out on bail in Kelowna, was that frequently I was required to make an appearance in court. Following one such appearance as I walked from the courtroom I was served with another bunch of papers, which turned out to be a Civil Suit launched against me by Steven Lee! I had of course assumed I would be sued by him at some point, but had incorrectly thought it would come in an orderly fashion after the Criminal Suit was over. Well I was wrong, very wrong, and I had days to find a civil lawyer and respond to this new civil suit.To make matters as complicated and expensive for me as possible, Mr. Lee had filed the suit out of the Campbell River Registry, way up on Vancouver Island. I was totally ignorant of how the law functions, but my education, for which I was going to pay dearly, was just beginning!

I lived in four different places before finding semi-permanent lodging in Kelowna where I rented a ground level suite from a realtor friend. At least my family now had a place where they could come to visit and sleep over without imposing on friends or relatives.Carol and Dianne, would visited almost daily bringing Lesley and Lori, our two youngest girls with them. Sometimes Matthew and Phillip would come, but they had school to attend and paper routes to do, as well as house chores, so they often stayed at home. Our older children visited whenever it suited them.

I can't say how much it meant to have those visits with my kids, because I had become a displaced person... I could never go home again! God, what a feeling!

Meanwhile I contacted a local lawyer who filed my, "Statement of Defense"for the civil action in the Supreme Court of B.C. The half hour consultation and filing cost me a cool grand! Talk about a license to steal! I wasn't sure a local lawyer was the person to represent me and after a conversation with Mr. Jackson, my criminal lawyer, a decision was made to have one of his lawyer friends call me from Vancouver. Between those calls, I was served with more papers from Lee's lawyers, stating that they had successfully applied to the court to have all my assets frozen! This restrained me from raising any money to defend myself by selling any of my assets! My first thought was.... How could this be? How could I pay the lawyers fees and defend myself? I must be allowed to raise money by selling my home!When Ritchie Clark,(Mr. Jackson's lawyer friend)called, I explained my dilemma to him. He responded that the first order of business was to have the Mareva judgment lifted, which was restraining me from selling assets! He went on to explain that having him represent me in the civil action wouldn't hurt either, as he and Brian would be able to share information between them.

Anyone having serious dealings with the legal system knows how much faith they must have in their legal representatives. **The faith you place in your lawyer is directly proportional to the gravity of the offence!** I was in this mess up to my neck; perhaps over my head, and I needed the best lawyers I could afford to save me. If I was unsuccessful in defending against these charges, I was headed for a federal penitentiary! In addition I would lose my job, my pension, and only God knew what would befall my family!?

I was scared….. Really scared, and for those of you who are thinking I deserved it, you may be right….. Maybe….. But my good wife and children didn't! I won't start making any excuses yet, and I must admit, **no person in their right mind goes after another person with a twelve gage shotgun!**

My realtor listed our home for sale, as Mr. Clark prepared an application for the court to have the recent restraining judgment against me lifted. I set about raising as much money as possible to pay the legal fees. There were civil and criminal lawyers in Vancouver to pay, as well as a local law firm who faxed papers to Campbell River for me to be presented by another lawyer that represented me whenever an appearance in court was necessary! This was unbelievable!I began to default on mortgage payments, but my bank continued debiting my current account. Even though I only had overdraft protection for five hundred dollars, the bank just kept debiting my account? I never understood how they could do this, but when the amount reached six thousand dollars, I began to hear from them. Eventually I was served with papers to appear in Court in Vancouver, which I didn't do probably because I simply couldn't handle the stress. The bank got a judgment against me and I just added it to my pile of bills.I have never defaulted on a debt in my life, but I can say it would have been much easier for me had I just thrown in the towel and declared bankruptcy! The reason I never took that action was because I believed I had incurred those debts and should honor my word by paying them off! At times I found the stress of my situation unbearable…. Each knock at the door… each ring of the telephone seemed to bring more bad news!

Each month I was required to make an appearance in court on the criminal charges as we moved towards a hearing. One month I failed to make an appearance as Mr. Jackson understood erroneously that my presence wouldn't be required.Later that morning people were running up to me at work saying they had heard on the news the police were looking for me because I had failed to appear in court! …Wow!…that was unnerving as I fought back panic found a phone and called Mr. Jackson in Vancouver.Brian working in conjunction with Crown Counsel finally got the whole mess straightened out, and satisfied the Court by having me make an appearance shortly thereafter! I was a nervous wreck because I never knew what to expect from Mr. Lee, his legal representative, the media, the legal system in general or even my own legal team!

Mr. Clark had gotten the Mareva judgment restraining me from selling my assets lifted, and I could now sell our home. This made all the lawyers happy, as they love holding your money in trust, when they have first claim on those funds! When our property was sold, mortgage paid off and other expenses taken care of, the balance of the money was sent to Mr. Clark's law firm of Devlin Jensen, to be held in trust.I was relieved that I had some money with which to pay the lawyers. Carol and I had a meeting with Brian Jackson and Ritchie Clark in Vancouver and told them that when the trust funds ran out we were flat broke, our house was gone and we had nothing left!

Carol found a house in Kelowna with a suite in the basement for rent. She and the kids took the upstairs and Dianne took the basement suite. It was wonderful for them to finally get away from Stephen Lee, but difficult for Carol to leave her home of fifteen years! The church family at Westbank Bible Chapel pitched in and moved Carol, the kids, and Dianne as well. What a load off my shoulders this was as I wasn't allowed to return to my former home in Westbank. The move went very well as the Lee's could be seen peeking out their windows at all the people packing everything up next door.

The months following the shooting incident had been extremely trying on our family! Changes in everyone's daily routine became the norm and some of us handled those changes better than others. Carol was an emotional powder keg; at times in a state of disbelief that any of this was real! Our lives had changed so dramatically and so abruptly…. She was forced to make so many decisions now as I was living in a small suite somewhere else in Kelowna. Carol blamed me for much of what had happened and barely a day went by when she didn't tell me what a mess I had made of things.I agreed with her, because I was so ashamed of what I had done! Shooting the neighbor, losing our home, our family being split apart, having to live in different places. Carol and I weren't getting along now as we fought about how we would pay the mounting bills and how to cope with all the new problems we were facing!

I believe now that Carol may well have been on the verge of a nervous breakdown if in fact she didn't have one….. And I wasn't far behind. I couldn't blame her for any of this ….. But, where were we to go from here? Desperate people do desperate things. One of our friends convinced Carol to file for separation with a lawyer. This would assure that she received her rightful portion of our remaining assets, in the event that Lee was successful in his legal action against me. At the same time she had to face the reality that the Court had forced us to live apart by (a) not allowing me to return to our home in Westbank, forcing me to live elsewhere; and (b) Granting the Mareva judgment, restraining us from selling any of our assets.

It was explained to her that she would then be entitled to apply to Social Assistance for help with her rent payments. This whole mess was so complicated and distasteful to Carol that the very sight of me was often all it took to set her off ! Against her will but in order to save a small portion of our remaining assets she saw a lawyer and filed for separation! She dutifully went and explained her predicament to Social Assistance and did get monetary assistance from them! I cannot express how difficult this was for her to do, the shame she endured because of my actions! She was forced to do all these things that she never believed in just to secure a small portion of our remaining assets which she was more then entitled to under the law! A mother of eight children, a devout Christian woman of forty eight years forced to go hat in hand to welfare through absolutely no fault of her own!!

As for me I had lost basically everything with all my cash now being held in trust by the lawyers. I had been planning an early retirement by age 55 with no mortgage and a suite in our home for extra income ...... life would have been perfect. All that had changed; in an instant, now and forever... our lives had changed. **The best laid plans of mice and men...gang aft agley!**

The preliminary hearing in my criminal case was held in Kelowna, Sept.06/07, 1995.(the date of our 27th wedding anniversary) what a gift! My lawyer, Mr. Brian Jackson attended, did his thing, and spent some time in the evening getting acquainted with the Demers family. We managed a bicycle ride and he demonstrated his magnificent abilities with a yo-yo! It was determined by the Court that there was sufficient evidence presented by the crown requiring a trial. Was there ever any doubt that this case was going to trial? Brian simply commented at the end of the hearing that he was satisfied, said he'd be in touch and returned to Vancouver.I must confess that I was feeling pretty depressed with everything in general. There were moments when I felt like giving up..... Just throwing in the towel! Thank God that at those times a friend would call, or I'd get a friendly pat on the back which bolstered my moral and helped me to focus on the good not the bad! I want to relate one miracle that Carol and I experienced just after the hearing.

Carol received a visit from Doreen and Fred Bellis. Fred was a co-worker of mine on the Westbank Telephone crew, and Doreen was his good wife, and a registered nurse. As they were leaving Carol's house, Fred casually mentioned to

Carol, " Oh, we left a little something for you on the kitchen counter", and away they went. Fred's parting remarks were made so nonchalantly that Carol soon forgot them and busied herself with household duties.

Later that evening, I paid a visit to Carol and the kids and she greeted me at the door and asked me to sit down with her. She became very somber as she related the events of the Bellis's visit and with trembling hand passed me the envelope they had left for us.As I opened the envelope to read the card inside a cheque for **ten thousand dollars fell into my lap!** As I read the words of comfort and tried to grasp the reality of the cheque in front of me, my eyes filled with tears. Tears of gratitude but also of incredulity at this real act of compassion! Carol and I were overwhelmed with the generosity of these people...... a moment which will live with us forever! **(But this is only the beginning of the miracle!)** I'll skip ahead a bit to the trial.........

In April, 1996, we went to trial, scheduled to last for three weeks. My lawyer, Brian Jackson had booked the necessary time off from his Vancouver law practice, as he would of necessity be required to be in Kelowna full time as he focused all his efforts on defending me.Preliminaries were completed, the jury sworn, and the court recessed for lunch. Upon returning from lunch, the court was reconvened and the judge addressed everyone present that he had a dilemma on his hands! During lunch one of the jurors had sent him a note asking to be excused on the grounds that her son's father in law (**Fred Bellis**) had worked with me for 15 years! She stated that she had so much information about this case from family that she was prejudiced and couldn't render an impartial decision!

The judge's dilemma was that the jury had already been chosen and sworn, and he now felt that he had no alternative but to call a **Mistrial!** The judge advised that while an attempt could be made to recall the pool of people from which the jury had been chosen, he was not optimistic. As the judge completed his announcement of a mistrial my lawyer whispered in my ear, " **This just cost you, ten thousand dollars"**! Brian was dead serious, as there was no way he could have anticipated something like this happening and would now have to reschedule his practice as preparations were made for a new trial! Brian Jackson had no knowledge of the ten thousand dollar gift that Doreen and Fred had given us! Fred Bellis had no knowledge that his daughter's mother in law would be the cause of a mistrial.... Thereby costing me ten thousand dollars! Someone knew however....... And I leave it to you to draw your own conclusions!

Carol and Dianne received notice that the house they were living in was to be sold, which meant they had to look for another place to live. Dianne decided to ask her father for the down payment which he gave her and a realtor friend found her a lovely unpretentious home with a nice suite up in the Dilworth area.In early October of 1995, Carol and kids (Mark, Matthew, Phillip, Lesley and Lori) moved in upstairs and Dianne took the suite downstairs. Dianne was the new landlord and you couldn't have asked for a better person for that job! The home, on Dilworth Mountain was centrally located in Kelowna and close to everything!

David came to live with me in the suite I was renting from my realtor friend. While Carol and the kids still came to visit, there were unresolved problems between the two of us and much underlying hostility towards me which could surface without warning turning into a whole scale argument. It was fortunate for all of us that Carol and I had separate living quarters at the time, as it gave both of us a place to cool off, to reflect on where we'd go from there.

After much discussion and argument Carol made a decision to apply for work. She knew as did I, that we simply needed more money to handle all the bills. While she was reluctant to go back on the oath she had sworn twenty years earlier, when we left Dawson Creek, she knew it was a necessity. Carol got a job as a cashier at London Drugs and recently celebrated her tenth anniversary of employment there! It wasn't easy for her at first, as she experienced first hand the questions and gossip from staff who openly wondered if she was related to Darwin Demers. She found herself having to deal with many of the same problems I had experienced at work. The gossip, the insinuations, and sometimes the sarcasm of staff who had already made up their minds about my guilt.

To Carol's credit she proved the quality and integrity of her character to her co- workers who came to respect her. They came to know her as a hardworking mother of eight children. A Christian woman that never spoke badly of anyone, yet when asked gave honest answers about her opinions.

She was cheerful at work in spite of the burdens she bore, and confessed to me at times that it proved therapeutic for her to return to work, as it took her mind off her trouble at home.

One day Brian called to tell me the trial date had been set for April 1996. He went on to say that he would arrange some meetings for me with several doctors of psychiatry and sociology within the next few months. When the interviews with Dr. Lohrasbe and Dr.Ley were held in Vancouver, I had no idea what to expect. The only advice Brian gave me was to answer all their questions truthfully. I was given many tests, and of course asked many questions concerning every aspect of my life. There was nothing left untouched concerning my complete life history, which I was in no way prepared for. The meetings took place over a three day period and I was more than happy to return home when they were over. The meetings seemed so clinical to me, so devoid of empathy…. Perhaps that's the way it should have been.

Dianne and Carol had come to Vancouver to keep me company and they had their own questions for Brian as well.

They did some shopping and we did a little sightseeing and took in a movie at the Imax. Just before we left, Brian had a short meeting with Carol and I and stated that he wanted a cheque for 36,000.00 deposited in his account two weeks before the trial. I couldn't help but feel that what was a life and death situation for us was simply business for Brian. To be fair however he was doing his very best in a professional way for us and we were grateful. Back to Kelowna we went, resuming work and waiting to hear.Eventually I received a call from Brian saying he was satisfied with the way things had gone with the doctors and he felt we had a reasonably good defense. He would call me when the trial date was set and he would be coming to Kelowna to interview some character witnesses, around Easter.

I got a new job splicing with B.C. Tel. which allowed me the freedom of working outside again. No longer would I be under the microscope of four hundred people in one office building. I would be reporting to the Penno Road compound, which housed, Construction, Installation & Repair, Splicing and the Mechanics departments. There were about a hundred people working here, mostly guys, many that I knew.With some trepidation I reported to my new position on a Monday morning and as I walked through the door was greeted with **"Shooter's here"**! followed by a hearty laugh. The guys were sitting around tables shooting the breeze as they waited for their work assignments, when I arrived. They knew I was coming, the ice had been broken, and from now on I was one of them. Shooter, was my new nickname and became quite popular for a lengthy period, but gradually subsided. None of the supervisors really liked me being called Shooter, but most said nothing as they didn't want their crews to single them out as not having a sense of humor.

Easter arrived and with it Brian Jackson to interview character witnesses for the defense. One of the things Brian said to Carol as he stood on her rear deck taking in the view from Dilworth Mountain, was, " Carol, this is a father knows best neighborhood". He went on to confide in her that he felt things were progressing well with the legal case. Brian used Dianne's suite to conduct his interviews with all the character witnesses, as it was a private place he was able to call each person to and speak with.Brian did ask Carol if she and I were planning on reconciling and she replied she was hopeful. I must say I was hopeful as well and within a month that hope became reality! Our son David, continued renting John's suite and I moved into the house with Carol and the kids. I was given a bedroom of my own...... but it was a start!

Funny how life goes as our renter had become our land-lord! Dianne still had the suite downstairs, while Mark, Phillip and I had a couple of the bedrooms downstairs on Carol's side of the house. We were now almost completely reunited as the family we had been before the shooting incident in Westbank sixteen months earlier.Our new home on Dilworth Mountain saw me keeping a low profile as the trial approached. The family next door to us had three kids that got along very well with our children..... Thank God! It didn't hurt that their dad and I worked together at B.C. Tel. either. Just across from us lived another company employee as well which really did help put me at ease. The last thing I needed was any trouble with the neighbors once they realized who their new neighbor was.

I became apprehensive as the date of the trial approached and at times felt like getting into my car and driving off into the sunset. The words of my lawyer at our first meeting continually rang in my ears, **You're going to do time"**! I was afraid..... I honest to God couldn't imagine anything worse then going to jail; yet I lived with the dread each day that jail was where I was going. For the past year and a half I had heard a goodly number of jail jokes, even laughed at them, but inside I was really scared ! I don't know how true the stories about Aids and HIV are, but I didn't want to find out doing my own research.

The day before the trial was scheduled to begin, Brian and his young associate Michael Bain arrived. We had managed to rent a home for the lawyers for a month as it was the most economical way for us to go. The evening was spent interviewing my boys and some of their friends from the old neighborhood as well as myself, in preparation for the second half of the trial. I headed home around 10:pm that evening with fear and trepidation as I thought about what the morning would bring. Tomorrow was day one of a three week criminal trial which would determine how the rest of my life would be lived!~

Chapter Six

Sing Another Prairie Tune

—ɯɯ—

After a year and a half working as an installer- repairman apprentice for B.C. Telephone I became homesick. The girls I had met here only served to remind me of Carol, who by now was attending Baptist Leadership Training School in Calgary. I wrote to Sask. Tel. gave a brief history, and applied for a job. Within a month I was advised there was a job waiting for me one hundred miles from Prince Albert in North Battleford,Sask. I was told I would be transferred to P.A. as soon as a position became available. En route to Saskatchewan, I stopped in Calgary to visit Carol. It was a short visit but a good one with a hint of better things to come.

I think I made history heading East to work for a telephone company as most people wanted to work in B.C. I had forgotten how cold it gets in Saskatchewan! It was so cold you would start a ground rod in mid February from a stepladder with a ground rod pounder and return to finish it after the ground thawed in the spring! The ground there could freeze to a depth of eight or nine feet.

My transfer came through to Prince Albert in January and I was assigned to work in the "Special Services" department with Merle George, a good humored guy who handled all the switchboard installs and repairs. This was all inside work in the business community of P.A. The temperature was perfect all year round inside,and the work was of a far more complex nature then what I had been doing as an installer repairman. Although I enjoyed working in Special Services, it was in this department that I learned my technical limitations. Some of us just don't have the smarts for certain types of work and it didn't take me long to realize that I would never be quite proficient enough to handle this job on my own! Sure I was young and just apprenticing and under the watchful eye of a journeyman in most cases capable of performing the work. It's just that you get a feeling about things and I just don't think I had the smarts for that position.

I was home at last boarding at mom and dad's and getting reacquainted with old friends. Carol came home and landed a job with Sask. Tel as an operator. I was happy when we started dating again, this time on a more serious level. Carol's parents weren't crazy about her dating me though, as they thought I was a little too wild a guy for their daughter. They were always telling Carol that she could do much better, and they were right, she could have done much better!

The summer of 67, a band I had seen featured at the P.N.E.(summer 66) was playing out at Emma Lake doing the resort circuit. The group called " The Guess Who" had really impressed me so I invited my close friend Dan Holuk, his sister Donna, her friend June, and Carol to go and see them.There weren't fifty (50)people at that dance all night and that includes **Randy Bachman, Burton Cummings, Jim Kale and Garry Peterson**. To their credit they put on a fabulous show, demonstrating that they were consummate professionals. Even at that early stage in their careers "The Guess Who" proved they had everything it takes to be great! I would have given anything to have been able to play with a band of that caliber!

After the show we talked with a very despondent drummer, Garry Peterson. He said they had recently returned from England, that they owed a lot of money and if the band didn't get a break pretty soon they were probably going to quit. Many promoters had made promises to these guys which were never kept! They really were a dejected looking group that evening and who could blame them?It's hard to believe isn't it, that this group which went on to become the very best band in Canada, ...**almost didn't!**"The Guess Who" did a reunion tour across Canada last summer and I saw the show in Kelowna, B.C. Thirty five years later they are better than ever. It was impossible to get to talk to them here, but speaking for myself, I'll never forget the exclusive show they gave us that night at Emma Lake!

Danny Holuk, (my best friend) was in his second year university studying pharmacy and Warne Soyland was studying veterinary medicine, both in Saskatoon. Carol and I were pretty serious about marriage, but her parents knew she had met another boy at B.L.T.S in Calgary and hoped she would end up with him instead!Carol finally suggested to me that if I returned to B.C. and got rehired with B.C. Tel. she would come out and marry me! I agreed, knowing how her parents felt I didn't see much chance for us if we didn't get away from P.A. for a good long while.

I gave my notice to Sask. Tel with a fair degree of trepidation; I was leaving a great job with a secure future, and no prospects at the other end! I have since learned that Sask. Tel. hasn't laid anyone off since the company's formation in 1903! I wonder how many companies, American or Canadian that can make that claim?

Chapter 7

Go West Young Man Again

—ᘳᘰᘵ—

I set my sights on trying to get a job with B.C.Tel and headed for Vancouver, B.C. arguably the most beautiful city in Canada! My cousin Dennis Demers, was enrolled at Simon Fraser University, located atop Burnaby Mountain, a subburb of Vancouver. Dennis was living in residence there so I reasoned this would make a good place for me to live while I looked for work.I found him with no trouble and he suggested to me that perhaps I should consider going over to the University of Victoria, where he had enrolled for the upcoming year. The plan was that I would go to Victoria using his name, while he would stay at "S.F.U." and no one would be any the wiser!...Hmmm... It might just work even though Denny is a genius and ....well we already established that I was special! In actual fact my I.Q. is somewhere around room temperature. After giving the idea some thought, I decided that I would try to get back on with B.C. Tel. but I must say I was tempted.

768 Seymour Street was the main headquarters for B.C. Tel. in 1968 and that's where I went, hoping to be rehired for a second time. The company had a steady stream of people from all over the world, coming in for job interviews with

it's large personnel department. Suddenly the reality of who I would be competing against hit me! Two weeks after my first interview I was still waiting.... in a fit of desperation, I walked into an armed forces recruiting station and wrote some entrance exams. After passing all the tests I was scheduled for a physical which I also passed and a date was set for me to report to the Air Force!

If I was desperate before, I was panic stricken now, and I returned to the B.C. Tel. office determined to try one last time. The answer was the same as before; there was nothing for me right now. The guy I had been pestering for the past three weeks to a month, was sympathetic and patient, but didn't know what he could do for me? Finally I asked him if he would do me a favor and call Mr. Jinkerson, in Prince George and tell him I needed a job? I related how Mr. Jinkerson had once told me (at a party) that if I ever needed a job to give him a call. I knew this was a last ditch attempt at trying to get on with the telephone company and that it was a feeble attempt at best, but, what else did I have?; if this didn't work I was going into the air force!?

There were a number of reasons at that point why I should have been unsuccessful. Mr. Jinkerson could have retired; moved; died; forgotten saying anything to me or even remembered who I was. The human resources guy could have pretended to make the call and not bothered, and I would never have known the difference, but that's not what happened! The call was made and Mr. Ray Jinkerson told personnel to send me up to Prince George, for some expense money, after which I could proceed up to Kitimat, where the whole town was being converted to dial telephone service. I don't know who was more incredulous!; me or the man in human resources who had placed the call? I was going to be lodging at "Skogland Hot Springs Resort" fourteen miles past Terrace on Hwy 37,and I would be on full expenses to boot! **Remember, I said, Someone was looking after me!**

I had known some of the guys on this conversion crew in Kitimat, when I worked in Prince George back in 65/66. They welcomed me and quickly introduced me to the rest of the telephone family.Construction had placed new cable in Kitimat and were completing the splicing. Now it was time for our crew of installers to rewire each house from the terminals in; install a dial telephone over which a test call was placed. Once the new line facilities had been tested all the way from the central office to each home the dial tone was removed until the night of the cutover. The procedure was time consuming, and when completed would displace approximately one hundred operators, providing customer dialing.

In addition to the pressure from her parents, a boyfriend from her days at B.L.T.S. had been calling Carol from Calgary, trying to persuade her to come to university there. Carol had been talking with him for the past year, and he made a visit to P.A. and told her that as soon as he finished university, (7 years) they could be married. It wasn't meant to be and she made the decision to come to B.C. and marry her highschool sweetheart!We were married September 07, 1968 in St. Matthews Anglican Church in Terrace, B.C.

My new wife and I set up house in a one bedroom basement suite on Grebe Street in Kitimat. It rains fairly steadily in Kitimat in the fall,(100 plus inches per year) until it turns to snow (30-40 ft.). There is no parking on the streets in winter as snow blowing equipment runs twenty-four hours a day! Children are warned to stay off the snow piles in their front yards as the risk of contact with power lines is a real concern.To people spending their first winter in Kitimat it was a real education learning how to deal with the sheer volume of snow that falls so rapidly. Everyone who has lived there has a story to tell such as being unable to locate their car after working an eight hour shift during a heavy snowfall! You set your alarm an hour early as your driveway would almost certainly have a foot or more of snow to shovel, before you could move the car. Once or twice a month it was a wise precaution to shovel off the roof.

In February it started to rain again, the snow disappeared and spring was upon you with sun and perfect weather before you knew it. Kitimat was the home of Alcan,(the Aluminum company of Canada) when I arrived and when I left the following year, Eurocan was constructing a large pulp mill there. Power was provided from the secure town site of Kemano, hidden among the tall mountain peaks, during World War Two, to protect it from bombing.A large percentage of the population in Kitimat came from Europe, specifically Portugal, Spain and Italy, although we made friends with very nice people from Ireland and Canada! It was a pleasure working and living with them as they were industrious, friendly, and just loved the telephone guys to sample their wines! We were always being given bottles to take home.

Kitimat is situated seventy miles inland, connected to the ocean by the Douglas Channel. There are many Salmon spawning streams in this area and of course the fishing is excellent! A sophisticated fishing fleet is located fourteen miles away at Kitimaat Indian Village, which we also converted to dial service at the same time.

There were many other people working for B.C. Tel. in Kitimat while we were preparing for the conversion to dial service. The large force of operators as well as regular employees who lived in town providing and maintaining normal day to day service, were all going to be affected in some way, by our work!There were over one hundred operators employed locally who would be displaced by the conversion to dial service as they would no longer be required to assist with local calls! The existing installer-repairmen, central office and radio men, as well as customer service representatives who lived and worked in Kitimat found their quiet pace of life dramatically impacted! When dial service came to a community it really was the end of an era and the beginning of another!Gradually the entire cut crew moved into Kitimat and supervisors for the crew came and went as well. We all chummed around together at times often with other friends and people of the community we got to know over the months we were there.

It was customary towards the end of the working day for the I&R crew (installation and repair crew) to grab a coffee, discuss the day's activities, make plans for the next day and just generally shoot the breeze. We then took off for the I&R compound located at the rear of the telephone office to park our vehicles. To access the rear of the office you first had to drive through a small public parking area, then along a narrow driveway which led to the rear of the building.As we arrived at the office, it was necessary to drive single file along the building to the I&R parking lot and then back into our designated spot. This procedure was repeated each day and tended to become an automatic reflex, due to it's repetition. At that time, we were driving heavy International pick-ups and the trucks with manual chokes and throttles. These trucks started well, had excellent traction and because of the manual throttle you could vary the engine speed up and down with engine temperature.

It didn't take me long to discover a trick if your front wheels got stuck in the snow. My idea was to put the truck in reverse, pull out the manual throttle and slowly release the clutch. I would allow the rear wheels to spin just fast enough so the engine wouldn't stall, get out of the cab and rock the truck until the rear wheels got enough traction to pull the truck out onto dry road whereupon the increased load would stall the engine! I used this trick successfully on several occasions and never had a problem of any kind. One midwinter day while parking our vehicles, my front wheels became stuck in the huge pile of snow surrounding the lot. The other guys were lining up single file waiting their turn to park, as I pulled out the throttle, set the rear wheels spinning, and exited the cab. I went to the front of the truck and leaned my back into it. I got the truck rocking and with a smug smile of satisfaction waited for the engine to stall as the rear wheels hit dry pavement.Just for a second I glanced at the guys watching and I swear that I saw their smiles change to looks of fear, **That truck took off, in reverse, with no one behind the wheel!** Each man watched with a stunned look of disbelief as my driverless vehicle accelerated across the lot! Some only half watched, while others shut their eyes tight hoping to blot out the reality of what was happening! I swear that truck was going twenty miles per hour in reverse when it ran smack dab into the only other parked vehicle on the lot; **my foreman's truck!**

I had a wonderful time after that; filling out accident forms in triplicate, trying to explain to a less than happy supervisor what I was trying to do? I got a couple of days in the park to think about it..... and all I can say is, it seemed like a good idea at the time! This accident report became widely circulated as kind of a funny story when accidents were reviewed at defensive driving courses. I don't think my name was ever used, but I'm not certain and I'm don't think it would have helped my career with the telephone company either! It really sounds like something Vedo would have done according to Ernestine, doesn't it?

My folks enjoyed their visit to Kitimat, when they came out for our wedding so much that dad applied for a job as purchasing agent for Eurocan Pulp, in Kemano. He had experience with book keeping from his hotel days, which he put to good use when his application was successful. Housing was provided as an incentive to work in Kemano, as it was fairly isolated. This gave dad a good income and the opportunity to save some money.So mom, dad and my little sister, Paula, moved to Kemano, B.C. from Prince Albert, Saskatchewan. B.C.Tel. looked after communications in Kemano, so I had several opportunities to visit with them. It was great to have my folks in B.C. as we could see them more often now. Eventually the Kitimat conversion came to an end and the crew moved out to the Hazelton area, to continue their work. I chose to stay in Kitimat until a position as an Installer-Repairman in Dawson Creek, became available. Carol and I made the move to Dawson, just prior to Christmas, and began work in early January.

My Uncle Wilf (Mom's younger brother) and his family, lived in Dawson Creek, so we would have some family there to help us get settled. Dawson is located in the Peace River country close to the Alberta border. Many large trucking firms were located there, transporting freight and supplies up and down the world famous," **Alaska Hwy**", built by the Americans. The population of Dawson Creek hovered around twelve thousand. The Peace River country is a major agricultural area dotted sporadically with oil and gas wells. The climate was severe and had four distinctly different seasons. We felt comfortable there in a very short time however, because the country was much like Saskatchewan.

Carol and I purchased our first home just before Christmas. It was a three bedroom, eleven hundred square foot, twelve year old home. Our cost was around eleven thousand dollars. Sure everything is relative, but it didn't require the combined income of husband and wife to handle the mortgage payment then! We were only twenty-one and buying our first home, which we felt was a significant accomplishment, when one considered our backgrounds.Carol got a job at Safeway as a cashier, which helped out financially and gave her something to do.We settled in building our lives together and getting to know people in the community over the next several years, when Carol finally became pregnant.

The big day arrived April 30, 1971 and off we went to the hospital with Carol's sister, Elizabeth(visiting) and I, at her side, right to the labor room.When the woman further along with her labor started to moan and groan, I politely excused myself not wanting to watch the same thing happen to Carol. I told myself that because her sister Elizabeth was there, that I wouldn't be needed, and politely excused myself ! What a coward I thought, as I headed for the waiting room! Carol managed beautifully without me, proof positive that I had made the correct decision in the first place! After twelve hours labor we became the parents of a baby girl and all I can say is it didn't hurt a bit! We named the baby Karyn Lynn Demers. She was a lovely little girl who took after her mother in many ways.

Eighteen months later daughter number two made her entrance into the world. Janice Carolyn Demers was a plump little redhead who took after her daddy.(the freckles would come later). The girls were great playmates for each other and the differences between them age wise disappeared in no time.Until I had my own I really never liked kids! I wonder how many men experience this phenomenon? At any rate those two little girls became our pride and joy!

Our work with B.C.Tel. involved basic installation and repair of residential and business telephone equipment in the towns of Chetwynd, Hudson's Hope, Ft. St John and Dawson Creek, as well as rural service around these towns. A rural party line could have up to ten customers on the line and be fifty miles away. As a result these lines were far more labor intensive than a private line, requiring a great deal of maintenance and driving on our parts. The driving hazards alone, on the thousands of miles of secondary and side roads, were intensified by the cold northern winters.When a trouble was reported on a party line and tested out towards the field it became the I&R Crew's responsibility to get that line repaired regardless of the weather! We were in and out of those trucks chasing and clearing troubles as they came in and each man had his share of accidents and close calls to talk about over coffee breaks.

I recall leaving Dawson one mid winter morning on a graveled road after a snow fall. The road had been freshly graded several feet over the sloping sides of the ditches on either side which gave the impression the road was wider than it was. The sky was overcast almost a whiteout, making for treacherous driving conditions, as it was difficult to see where the road ended and the ditch began. I had a fair distance to go before I would be able to start patrolling the open wire circuit that was in trouble, so while I was trying to exercise caution I also wanted to make the best time possible. Gradually I came up behind an old fellow trailing snow behind him and driving slower than me; Finally after following him for several miles, I pulled out to pass him. I was almost parallel to the old gentleman when my van's front left wheel caught the snow which had been graded flat out over the ditch, and at a speed of about fifty miles per hour I was pulled down into the ditch! I kept the wheels straight however and found myself driving down in the ditch, still parallel to the road, and still moving at about the same speed! snow was spewing over my windshield, but I kept the pedal to the floor and turned the steering wheel a little to the right. To my surprise the van edged it's way right back up on the road right behind the old fellow who as far as I could tell had missed the whole thing!

One day I got a call from my cousin Dennis, who was teaching school at the coast. One of his new hobbies was sailing, and he wanted Carol and I to take a sailing trip with him on our summer holidays. Denny convinced me that a one week in the Gulf Islands would be a wonderful holiday! We decided that August would be great sailing weather and Dennis began making the preparations. Dennis said he'd look after everything for us and all we had to do was find a sitter for the kids.

Carol's parents had moved to Kelowna, and they volunteered to baby sit our girls for a week. We drove our new

Buick wagon to Kelowna, left our girls with Grandma, and headed for Vancouver, where we spent the night with Dennis. The next morning we drove to the Hyatt Marina where our 29 ft. sailboat was waiting. Dennis and Susan, a teaching friend of his, had already provisioned the vessel, so the four of us boarded the vessel and headed out the Fraser River towards English Bay.What an adventure, I thought, as we reached the bay and raised the sails on "Campella" the boat we had leased! The sails snapped to attention as they filled with wind, and our boat became one with nature! Carol and I took much longer to " become one with nature" as we spent the next ten hours throwing up! Poor Carol, I wanted so much to help her as she was so sick, but I had no strength left to do anything but throw up! I can honestly say at that moment, had I the strength, I would have thrown myself overboard! Luckily Dennis had Susan to assist as ship's mate, because Carol and I were out of it!

We made 52 miles under sail that first day..... (52 miles of hell)! I resolved that at the first opportunity I would escape to land and walk home! Finally after what seemed an eternity we docked at a little place called, Half Moon Bay. Carol had made such a mess of the floor that Dennis had to pull most of the shag carpet out of the ship, rinse it in the water and hang it up to dry outside. The next morning Dennis and I took the dingy and went to one of the local stores for some supplies. As I was feeling much better I decided to give it one more day before permanently abandoning ship! We had breakfast, went for some fabulous showers at the marina and Carol agreed to try one more day of sailing before she left with me!

The second day was so much better as the two of us began to get our sea legs. The sun was shining, the wind was decent and I took over from Susan as First Mate. We headed up the Sunshine Coast towards Pender Harbor, with great expectations. To our amazement my wife and I really did begin to experience some of the joy of sailing that Dennis had spoken of. We docked in Pender, and headed up to a local marina and bar for a little sightseeing and refreshment. We sat down at a table and discussed the trip to this point and found there could be life after sea sickness! All around the room were autographed pictures of N.H.L. hockey players who had come there on fishing trips. Judging by the pictures, many had been extremely successful, landing trophy fish! As I sat at the table, I began to experience a type of motion sickness in reverse, although to a lesser degree. Apparently after getting one's sea legs.... which refers to the brain's ability to adapt to the roll, pitch, and yaw of the ocean; when at rest, the brain must reverse this procedure.

We finished the day sightseeing and relaxing at Pender Harbor, and prepared for day three. Our plans were to sail out towards Texada Island, then swing left around the North Western tip of the island and sail South through the Sabine Channel to Lasqueti Island, where we would rendezvous with Ken and Val Johnson, friends of my cousin. Ken, taught woodworking at a vocational school, and along with his wife,(Val) and his father, had built a beautiful 39 foot sailboat which had been featured in an issue of " Pacific Yachting" magazine. Val was a lovely marine biologist and a very talented cook as well! The Johnson's owned land on Lasqueti Island and were planning on building a home there sometime in the future.

The winds were strong in Georgia Strait, which made for great sailing weather. Carol and I were really enjoying ourselves by now as we began to experience the timeless tranquility of wind power! A real sense of peace enveloped us as we sailed along, oblivious to what was going on in the rest of the world! Aside from the sound of the wind filling the sails it was quiet and whenever we steered downwind, there was absolutely no sound whatsoever, as we became one with the wind.Every so often we passed other sailors and we would wave a greeting to each other as we shared this wonderful experience. Power boaters didn't seem as interested in waving, and we experienced a feeling of distain towards them as they passed with their noise and water pollution.

As we slipped into the Sabine Channel, a storm blustered upon us seemingly from nowhere and an 8 foot ground swell quickly developed as we experienced our first rough water.

Dennis released the tautness in the mainsail allowing it to luff, (flap freely)as he gingerly inched his way forward, preparing to pull the sail down and secure it from the wind. As he crawled towards the bow, we hit an 8 foot wave head on and then as the bow crested the wave we crashed straight down 16 foot to the bottom of the next oncoming wave. Dennis who was crawling by now found himself kneeling in mid air! Had Dennis fallen overboard at this point he would have been a dead duck and I don't know what would have happened to us! He grabbed for the lifeline surrounding the deck, and crawled back to us in the cockpit with an ashen look on his face! He knew he should have had a safety belt on attached to the lifeline circling the boat. Then had he been thrown from the deck he would have still been attached to the boat and we could have pulled him aboard! We were all very lucky..... this time.... no major catastrophe!Sails secure, we switched to diesel power and motored on towards the safety of Lasqueti Island. We had to arrive at high tide in order to clear the bottom of the narrow channel to be negotiated before reaching the sanctuary of the small inner harbor, where we were to rendezvous with the Johnsons.

The next morning we met Val and Ken and his brother Hal, an Edmonton policeman who was holidaying with them. It was decided that Val, Ken and Dennis would go scuba diving, while Hal and I would snorkel, and Carol and Susan would go hiking. The divers suited up and I grabbed my camera and started taking pictures. We tied our rubber dingy to the Johnson's motor launch and left our sailboats and headed out the channel to the dive site. We set a crab trap out on the way to the dive site and pulled six or so out for supper, on our way back . Meanwhile Susan and Carol had found an excellent place to dig for clams and had returned to the boat with a pail full. The clams were placed in a strainer and hung over the side of the boat to allow the sand to be washed out. A superb meal was being prepared from our days activities and we were having a great time collecting all the ingredients!

We arrived back at the boats and got washed and changed in preparation for our supper meal to be held aboard the huge Johnson boat. It was all so peaceful and relaxing as we were the only two boats anchored in this small harbor, which looked more like a little lake rather than a salt water port. We boarded the Johnson boat at 8:PM, where we were greeted by a lovely Val Johnson and her Persian cat " Blue". Picture two sailboats moored side by side, in little harbor, on a quiet moonlit night. It was as romantic as an evening on Bali in the movie " South Pacific"! I brought my camera and took pictures all evening as everything was just so magical that evening! We were given a tour of the superbly crafted boat the Johnsons had built, and the craftsmanship was of the highest quality! Val had utilized her culinary skills and prepared a salmon dish to compliment the fresh crab and clams and along with the drink and fellowship an unforgettable evening was enjoyed by all present!

The next morning we bid a fond farewell to our new friends and headed for Gibson's Landing. The weather was absolutely perfect for our sailing requirements and everyone aboard had an opportunity to handle the boat under Denny's able instruction. Time really does seem to stand still when you are sailing, or perhaps one just loses their perception of time? At any rate it is an extremely relaxing form of holiday. Arriving in Gibson's Landing we tied up to the main dock and headed up the steps towards land. As we reached the top we were greeted by the actual movie site of "Molly's Reach" where the famous " Beachcombers" series of the seventies was made! After taking pictures we continued on to town on foot until we found a restaurant, had supper, then just did some shopping. By the time we arrived back at the boat we were bagged and decided to hit the sack so we could get an early start back to Vancouver the following day.

The sun came up the following morning in all of it's crowning glory! Truly the last day of our sailing holiday was to be the most beautiful of all! I think the Sunshine Coast is among one of the prettiest areas of the world, especially when the sun shines, and today it was shining! Almost reluctantly we set sail and headed for Vancouver determined to cram as much sailing enjoyment into this final day as possible! I was shooting pictures of everything and Dennis was triumphantly posing in a prone position in the mainsail! We had the boat lying almost on it's side as we were racing along the water, skipping over the ocean like some flying fish! This was what sailing was all about!

As we approached the mainland it really was hard to tell exactly where we wanted to go. We knew approximately where we were, but not precisely! Somehow we had passed the North arm of the Fraser and didn't realize it. Inlets, streams, and the heavy population of buildings along the Vancouver coastline all served to obfuscate that little river we were searching for to access our inland marina.Our depth sounder began to act up indicating 14 feet, then 10feet, then 8 feet of water depth, which concerned us. Dennis was running from the cockpit to check the charts, then back again, with a puzzled look on his face when suddenly our boat lurched.... as if it had nudged something! We were completely surrounded by water and about three hundred yards from the shoreline, but we had definitely nudged.... something?! The girls were leaning over the side and shouting that they thought they could see bottom! As Dennis ran from the cockpit to the charts, trying to reconcile the discrepancies between the charts and our view of the shoreline a gust of wind caught his shirt and some cash ($115.00) flew from his pocket and out into the water! Dennis, jumped into the water right behind the money and managed to retrieve the hundred dollars, but the rest sank!

We quickly dropped our sails and almost as quickly the boat's bottom rubbed something again.... then again..... and we came to an abrupt stop! Dennis was incredulous as his mind refused to accept the obvious.... we had run aground! As the reality of what had happened, dawned on us, we became aware that our boat was beginning to tip over! The tide was going out and our boat was going over on it's side. I, abandoned ship on the high side of the boat and leapt out into five feet of water. Dennis, cranked the tiller to the side, grabbed a couple of paddles, jumped out on the low side and jammed them against the side of the boat to stop it from going over further. He then had the girls who were hanging on for dear life throw the anchors out from the high side, and we took them out as far as the ropes would allow and set them in the sand.

Dennis got on the radio and called for assistance from the coastguard, and then we set about gathering driftwood to further assist in stabilizing the boat. There we were walking around in less than two feet of water searching out pieces of wood to force against the boat's side and keep it upright! After about forty five minutes the coast guard was back on the radio telling us they couldn't locate us. Suddenly another voice came on the air inquiring of us if our mast covers were blue, to which we responded yes. The voice then continued, " Coast Guard, this is the observation tower at the Vancouver Airport. The " Campella" has run aground on the Iona Island sewage bank!" We were right next to the airport and were later told that dune buggies sometimes come down to motor on the sand dunes!

Within fifteen minutes we could make out the coast guard as they raced towards us in their jet boat. They had to walk the last hundred yards as the tide was receding so fast that we were now in about two feet of water! When the coast guard guys finally arrived we all had a good laugh as Dennis and one of them had had a similar experience on a sailing course they had been on. It's a small, small world!The coast guard assured us that everything Dennis had done since running aground had been done correctly, according to the book. "There was nothing to do now but wait for the tide to come back in", they said as they waved good bye and walked away pulling their jet boat behind them.

The girls decided to walk ashore and get the car, then meet us later at the Hyatt Marina. Dennis and I played chess on a sail boat tipped at a 14 degree angle as we waited apprehensively for the tide to return. Dennis said the tide could just as easily roll us over on our side as right us! What a joy it was as the boat ever so slowly began to right itself and eventually stand up and finally float!When we finally motored into port the girls were waiting with smiles of relief on their faces and we all had a good laugh about the day's activities. What a wonderful adventure it had been, with something in it for everyone! In fact Carol and I enjoyed it so much that we returned the following year for a similar vacation with Dennis!

The person Dennis had rented the boat from had been monitoring the radio and heard our whole ordeal with the coast guard and the airport live, as it happened. He was understandably upset and concerned about damage to his boat. However the whole episode had occurred on very fine sand and his boat was unscathed!Iona Island turned out to be located between the North and South arms of the Fraser River, so Dennis really hadn't missed our mark by much. It is funny to look at our pictures though and see our boat standing in a foot of water! We have had many a laugh over that incident over the years, but, that's life!

Carol and I said our goodbyes to Dennis the next day, and drove to Kelowna, to spend a week with her parents and our girls. Finally, after a wonderful holiday, the four of us drove home, to Dawson Creek. As nice as it is to go on holiday, I've always enjoyed coming home. The Peace River area is simply gorgeous as Indian Summer descends upon it. The kaleidoscope of colors are forever painted in my mind, but I cannot do them justice, on a page of black and white. The textures, the hues, the colors, and smells.... must be seen.... must be felt...must be absorbed!

There was an intermediate A hockey league operating in the Peace River country, which provided a lively source of entertainment for a lot of years. The Dawson Creek "Canucks"; Grande Prairie "Athletics" Ft. St. John "Flyers" and Hythe " Mustangs" represented their communities in this outlaw league.

More than one N.H.L. player sitting out a suspension played up in the "Peace" to stay in shape until his suspension was lifted.(hence the name outlaw league) Several retired (pro and semi pro) stars who had returned home, to the Peace, were coaxed out of retirement to play for their hometown teams. Hockey players such as Reg Kerr, Ed Diachuck, Lloyd Haddon, Jerry Lafond, the Joyal brothers, as well as many others, demonstrated their superb talents on the ice for all their hometown fans to see and discuss over coffee the next day!

We had moved to a new home in Dawson Creek, which we were very fortunate to buy on my salary. The house was a California ranch style, designed and lived in by an architect, and his family. It was a unique home of cedar, lots of glass and Swedish tile floors. There were all kinds of built ins, such as a herbal garden incorporated as a part of the extraordinary teak kitchen counters, and a complete wall of stained glass windows, in the dining room. It was a gorgeous home for its time and place, designed by a talented architect!

Carol and I decided it would be nice to have a boy, although it may have been my idea, I do know I really wanted a son. Carol loved children as she had been a playground supervisor as a teenager and had considered a post secondary occupation working with youth. Above all she was proving to be a great mother and she supported my idea agreeing that one more child was fine with her. She did say a boy would be nice, but the important thing was that the child be healthy.

Our son David, was born April 18th, 1977, and I cried! They were tears of joy at God having answered my not so silent prayer! Oh, David would be very special to me, but I was to learn that he would be just as special to his mom and sisters as he was to me! I can remember the first day that Carol brought him home from the hospital and while she was changing him, he peed right in her face! Having a son was going to be a new experience.

Bill and Annette Lexstrom were our neighbors, and as I worked with Annette we eventually became friends. The Lexstroms and their two boys Jeff and Blair began skiing as a family and invited us along. Carol and I really enjoyed skiing but with three little ones at home that required looking after, often she would stay at home and I would go with the Lexstroms. Bill was a very strong man with a robust love for life and a wonderfully impish sense of humor. Although he was eight years my senior I never really noticed the age difference as his zest for living made him seem much younger than he was! He was a talented welding instructor at the local college and later started his own welding and fabricating shop in Dawson Creek. He also purchased a couple of semi transports which he put to work on the Alaska Highway, hauling freight.

The Lexstroms had Dobermans and we had German Shepherds and after kicking the idea around for sometime Bill and I decided it would be fun to take our male dogs to a dog show in Edmonton. Bill had been fabricating a two stall dog trailer at work and completed it just in time for a spring show. We loaded up the trailer with our two males, and the car with Jeff, Blair, Bill and I and headed for the dog show in Edmonton. After arriving in town and getting our motel for the weekend we decided to take the dogs for a brief walk and pee break before bed. My dog did his business outside, but Axel, Bill's Dog didn't have to go, so we took him into the motel room with us, hoping he wasn't getting sick! Axel soon relaxed, lifted his leg and dropped at least two quarts of urine on the shag carpet in the middle of our living room! We all had a great laugh over this as there was little else we could do at the time but .... watch! The next morning it was off to the Kinsmen Field House for an interesting day of showing dogs. Bill and I both came back with ribbons from the show classes we entered, and we had a wonderful time with our dogs and Bill's boys. Jeff Lexstrom followed in his father's steps going on to become a welder in Dawson and Blair, the youngest went on to become a member of the Legislature with the provincial Liberal government!

During the mid 70's the city of Dawson Creek hired an engineer ,who condemned as unsafe our local curling and hockey arenas, and closed them down! This meant all the hockey teams (minor league, junior, intermediate) would have to find other rinks to play on. There would be no indoor rink available for figure skaters or fans of any ice sport at all! In addition absolutely no curling would take place in D.C. at all until the curling rink was made safe!Several local businessmen and building contractors were able with local politicians to come up with an acceptable fix for the curling rink, however no such luck with the Dawson Creek Memorial Arena. It would stay closed for the entire winter!It was a hardship on the local hockey teams having to play their at home games at arenas located out of town. As spring arrived no solution had been found to the arena problem, but a rumor that city council was going to build a new complex began to circulate. Many businessmen and builders felt that this was premature and a much cheaper solution could be found.

These people called several public meetings and eventually formed a group called "The Save The Arena Committee", which I joined. They proposed digging some test holes around several of the support columns where test samples of the concrete footings would be taken; tested by a reliable engineering firm and appropriate repair recommendations concerning the piers and footings considered as soon as possible.For some reason the city council and the mayor would not even consider this suggestion and in fact decided to demolish the Dawson Creek Memorial Arena! The battle lines were drawn, City Council vs. "The Save The Arena Committee". As council gave first, second, and third readings to a demolition order, the committee began digging their test holes and hired an engineering firm to test concrete samples. At the same time both sides waged a very public war of words using all the news media, and every forum available to them!

As the battle intensified, the community became polarized as public opinion was split more or less right down the middle. The petitions, debates, and discussions took their toll on the community, as friends and relatives found themselves on opposite sides of the debate.Finally the engineering firm hired by the "Save The Arena Committee" submitted their report which determined that in fact the arena could be repaired for a very reasonable amount! When the report was made public the pressure brought to bear on city council became unbearable and a decision to repair the arena was reluctantly made! It was a victory for our committee and for the taxpayers of Dawson Creek as well.

The fallout from the battle saw the entire city council along with the mayor replaced over the next two elections by members who had served on our committee! I myself ran for office in both elections, but was unsuccessful! That fall the Dawson Creek Memorial Arena was once again opened for the enjoyment and delight of the citizens of the community! This was my first real experience with participatory democracy! Being on the winning side is exhilarating, but being on the right side is more important to me! In any debate such as this people's feelings do get hurt and it takes time for cool headed thinking to return. It was quite some time before everything returned to normal in Dawson Creek and for some people, life there was never the same again!

About this time my friend Bill Lexstrom was taken ill with lung cancer. It took six months for that dreaded disease to take Bill's life! He was a powerfully built man and it broke my heart to watch him waste away so quickly! Smoking was the likely cause of Bill's cancer, which prompted Annette and I to take in a stop smoking clinic at the local hospital. Annette stopped smoking..... I did not! I finally managed to stop smoking in 1990, after thirty three years! I was smoking three packs a day when I finally quit. My advice to smokers who want to stop is to never give up trying and eventually you will succeed!

Chapter 8

To Farm Or Not To Farm

—ᔐᔑ—

As time passed I grew bored with my life, and whether it was wanderlust, the lack of adventure, or perhaps wanting to realize my full potential, I'm not certain..... I accepted an offer from my sister's husband Bert Harman, to go into the egg business with him in Saskatchewan. My brother in law, proposed that along with two other share holders, we would purchase two grading stations, "Star Egg Company" in Saskatoon and Regina; "Starline Farms" (35,000 layers, 17,000 chicks) in Saskatoon, and the Saskatchewan portion of "Miller Hatcheries".

This was an ambitious undertaking, with great potential for all of us, and I wanted to be part of it! Carol was reluctant.... to put it mildly! She had a beautiful home, three children and a life she was content with. She made it clear to me after six months of coaxing, that she would go, but not happily and never again would she work out side the home!

Bert put together a business plan, secured the necessary financing, submitted the proposal to the Saskatchewan Economic Development Corporation, (Sedco) and before we knew it we were in business! Bert was an extremely bright business man as well as a hard worker, who never asked anyone to do a job on the poultry farm he hadn't done himself. John Paley,one of the original owners and manager of Miller Hatcheries would stay with us, and continue to manage the Miller Hatcheries outlet in Saskatoon. Bob Schultz, manager of Star Egg grading station in Regina, would now be a part owner and continue managing that end. Bert, in addition to the layer operation he owned in Prince Albert, would now drive to Saskatoon each day to learn the management of Star Egg grading, which John would assist with. I was to manage and live on "Starline Farms", twelve miles out of Saskatoon.

Our home was sold, I gave my notice to B.C. Tel. and it was off to Saskatoon with our three kids to begin our new lives as farmers! I don't blame Carol for being unhappy, as I wasn't just leaving a good job, but a career.... for an uncertain future! Carol had given up her gorgeous home, uprooted the kids, said good bye to her friends, so I could chase my dreams of .... what? At the time I thought it was a good idea, getting into a business where my ideas counted; raising our children on the farm, having more input into the quality of produce they consumed. I've always been a romantic and perhaps I was simply trying to live a dream that wasn't realistic. I did have a feeling that this was my big opportunity to become wealthy! Maybe that's the real reason I was going into the egg business.

Carol and I rented a lovely home from John Paley,(one of my new partners) while we had the house at "Starline Farms" completely refinished. New cupboards, flooring, painting, and bathrooms, made the farm house livable. When Bert and I had looked the business over before buying it, the house had been completely forgotten. This sounds strange now, but I guess we were more interested in barns, cages and birds, at the time as these factors directly affected business.

Carol's brother and sister in law, Tommy and Betty Fusick, had recently moved to Saskatoon and they gave us a welcome hand with the house cleaning and stripping the old wallpaper off the walls of the living room! Tommy was managing a carpet store in town and gave us some excellent bargains on new carpeting. The rumpus room downstairs wound up with a wall completely done with free carpet samples! It made quite a visual statement as well as being a great sound room for my stereo.

As manager of "Starline Farms" I needed staff, which I set about finding the first day I set foot on the place. Bert had given me his ideas on what to look for, and his experience in this area was indisputable. Within a week I had eight teens (14 to 16) from nearby farms to call on. I needed the kids for part time work, such as flock changes, debeaking, unloading boxcars of foam egg cartons, major barn cleanouts and other tasks. The farm had been neglected, and there was a great deal of work to be done everywhere you looked. Barns needed painting, new ventilation was required to remedy the condensation problems in the barns, insulation had to be brought up to standards, maintenance and repairs to all machinery on the place was required!

When I had previously viewed the farm it must have been through rose colored glasses! After a month on the place and seeing all the problems that had to be rectified.... I can remember standing behind one of the barns and just crying my heart out!... What had I done? ....What had I been thinking, leaving such a lovely home and great job in Dawson Creek?!.... I couldn't tell Carol..... I must put on a brave face, and never let on I had just made the biggest mistake of my life! The automatic egg gathering system had fallen into such a state of neglect that it was cost prohibitive to repair. I hired three women from nearby farms to handle the daily routine of egg gathering. Only two would be required each day and I let them work out which hours and days during the week they wanted to work. The kids I hired would come for an hour after school each day and do full days on the weekends. Finally I needed one hired hand to assist me with all the regular chores and maintenance that a poultry farm with 35,000 layers and 17,000 replacement chicks requires. I found a single, Christian man first week, who rolled up his sleeves and went right to work.

With the house livable, though not completed, it was time to move Carol and our three children to the farm. I had been driving about 20 miles to work then back each evening and was tired of that. Star Egg Company had two large trucks used for moving eggs which were kept at the farm and as a result available to me to use on the weekends. We chose a Saturday morning and my farm boys supplied all the manpower needed to get the move completed.The Demers family took up residence at "Starline Farms" in midsummer of 1978. The kids loved the farm and never seemed to want for something to do.Bert had given me a large German Shepherd cross dog to patrol the farm and this dog(Rex) became my son's best friend. The two of them would play for hours, David on his bike and Rex just tagging along pestering him for attention every chance he got! Rex never strayed from the farm seeming to know what his responsibilities were from the moment he arrived. He kept the skunks and rats on the move whenever David wasn't around to play with. One of his greatest delights was to run for through the sprinkler whenever it was on. He would leap in the air like a puppy yelping ecstatically as the pulsating water soaked his heavy coat!

Karyn and Janice made friends with the Fraser boys, twins who lived on an acreage just down the road from us. We became friends with the Frasers, as our children attended school in Vanscoy and played together a great deal. Ron Fraser, was a city policeman and Danielle, his wife, an artist, who did pottery. Danielle took a course and rewired their home as they renovated it. As we went about settling in to farm life, Danielle was a real help to Carol sharing stories and information on the area; but more importantly listening to Carol as she poured out her heart about the life and home she had left behind! Danielle taught Carol to do pottery and made Carol's transition to farm life tolerable! As I look back on our experience on the farm I realize how important the Fraser family was to us in maintaining our sanity. Friends can make the life's difficult situations bearable. We visited back and forth, and went cross country skiing, but mostly just enjoyed our time together sharing life's simple pleasures.

We got to know many of the people on the surrounding farms especially the ones whose kids worked for us. They were really a great bunch and certainly made our lives in Saskatchewan enjoyable. Two or three times a year the staff of our farm would gather along with their families for a party and go swimming or out for a lunch, then return to the farm where we would visit, play music or even have the odd dance! These were the really good times we remember fondly whenever we reminisce about that period in our lives. The boys I hired were the best! I liked them all very much and depended on them a great deal. After school you would hear them coming to the farm on their motorcycles in the summer and their snowmobiles in the winter. I could never have operated that farm without them, but I don't recall if I ever came out and told them that? More importantly though they made the farm smile, along with the rest of the Demers family. I tried to thank them at times, but I'm not sure I succeeded. So to Chris, Dave, Sheldon, Dan, Stan, Kim, Kevin, the Kimptons and Hamiltons and their families, **thank-you, thank-you, thank-you!**

"Starline Farms" was located twelve miles Southwest of Saskatoon, on three hundred and forty acres of lightly treed gently rolling grassland. There was a house(1100 sq. ft.), four barns(40x180 ft. long), a large steel Quonset building, which housed a feed mill and a 2100sq. ft. freezer. In addition there were various buildings used for storage, a two stall garage and workshop with a bunkhouse and bathroom upstairs and an office down, plus an implement shed for tractors, etc.

The agriculture business was a complete departure for me from my normal line of work and I had a lot to learn about poultry farming in a hurry! There were several tractors on the farm and we were having trouble starting the one we used for turning the manure augers over during barn cleanout.One day I was cleaning a barn with a new hired hand Cecil, when the tractor driving the auger had to be refueled. Cecil drove over to the fuel tanks and I told him to fill the tank with the motor running as this tractor wasn't starting very well. He looked at me incredulously, but went about the job of gassing up obediently after I assured him I had done this several times with no repercussions.Cecil filled the tractor and as he lifted the gas nozzle out of the tank some fuel spilled out of the tank and down onto the hot motor block. Combustion was immediate and Cecil took off for the workshop where I was fixing something, hollering full volume for a fire extinguisher!

We grabbed two extinguishers and as fast as we could raced back to the fuel tanks where our little tractor was standing idling nonchalantly with a flame 5 feet high shooting from tank! With some trepidation we both approached the fuel tanks fearing that at any moment both of the 350 gallon diesel and gas tanks might explode. They didn't and we got the fire out, thank God!After apologizing to Cecil we both sat down kind of shaking and laughing at the whole experience as I had learned a valuable lesson and no real harm had been done. One week later, that little tractor was doing it's job, turning a manure auger at the chick barn we were cleaning. The tractor was idling nicely, it's p.t.o. turning the manure auger over which delivered manure out of the barn and into the manure spreader.Suddenly the little tractor exploded and burst into flames! Cecil came running with the terrible news that the tractor was totally engulfed in flames! We feared the barn catching fire and as our extinguishers were not yet back from being recharged,Cecil got a water hose from the chick barn and began soaking down the building next to the burning tractor, while I placed a hurried call to John Paley at Miller Hatcheries.

John had been talking to my brother in law Bert, long distance on another line when my somewhat panicky call came in. When I told him what was going on he told me to do my best and he would come as quickly as possible with some fire extinguishers. So John tore off for the farm and Bert sat on hold on the phone until John's secretary came on the line and simply told him that John would have to call him back as he had to rush out to Starline Farms to help Darwin put out a fire!Well you can imagine what was going on in Bert's mind as he tried to figure out what was happening! He called Carol, but she couldn't help him out as she was in the house and really wasn't aware of any fire. Everything seemed to be happening so fast and poor Bert who always prided himself in being on top of everything would have to wait and sweat, as his mind played all kinds of tricks on him about the fire at "Starline Farms".

When John finally arrived with the extinguishers he was so relieved to see that we had managed to contain the fire by hosing down the area of the barn next to the tractor. We extinguished the tractor fire and set about trying to figure out what had caused it in the first place. The tractor was a complete write off and we never did ascertain the cause of the fire. John's parting words as he left for town were, "I'm not going to die of old age Darwin, I'm going to die of fright!

A poultry operation of our size requires a great deal of work and the more modern the equipment the less labor is generally required. "Starline Farms" had not been maintained properly, in addition to which the caging systems were not state of the art. The end result was a labor intensive operation, lower productivity, with a poorer product. The house, the barns, the equipment, really were in a wretched state! Everything is paid for by the sale of eggs, so naturally the better your production and quality of product the more money is available for maintenance and the other problems which arise. The paradox is that unless you have well maintained modern equipment it is impossible to produce a high quality product at a volume which turns a profit!

An example would be the type of caging system the farm utilizes. A modern caging system such as "Cagemaster" (back in the mid 70's) used a white plastic cage superior to wire. The quality of the egg delivered to the egg room was much better as there were no wire marks on the eggs. Of course there are many other factors to be considered, but you get the idea.This system also had a manure belt under each of the three tiered levels of cages which meant that with the quick flick of a switch every row of cages could be cleaned very quickly with little effort! Many older systems are very labor intensive, requiring the scraping of manure boards on two levels each side into the waiting manure pit directly below by hand! From there a cable and blade system is used to move the manure to an auger trough which runs the width of the barns at the rear.There are other systems used but basically "Starline Farms" had the least modern equipment and in the worst of working order. Ultimately I found it impossible to deliver a high quality egg in the volume required to turn a profit!

One of my barns had a suspended two tiered wire cage system in it with a six inch manure pit underneath the cages, requiring cleaning once a week. The first month on the farm the door on this barn flew open, and two of the boys working in the barn raced towards me screaming, " the cages are falling, the cages are falling"! As soon as I calmed them down they were able to get me to understand that one whole tier of cages, of one row, had fallen into the manure pit! Not wanting to believe, them I headed for the barn to see just what had happened! To my utter dismay the boys had it absolutely right! The hooks holding the bottom tier of cages had pulled out of the ceiling at one end placing an unsupportable load on the next set of hooks, which pulled out. A very rapid domino effect brought the 120 foot row of cages, waterers, feeders and laying hens down into the manure pit!

I could hardly believe the sight my eyes were sending to my brain! What a horrible mess of cages and feed and birds and water and eggs and manure and ...... well my mind just didn't want to accept it! Now it was my turn to calm down; to get a grip on the feelings of panic threatening to engulf me! As cold and calculatingly as I could, I surveyed the damage, making notes and then headed for the phone to call my brother in law Chicken Man,(Bert Harman) for help. I tried to sound calm, cool and collected, but I don't think I was very convincing? Poor Bert, it seemed as if the only news that ever came from Starline Farms was bad news!After overcoming Bert's disbelief, we were able to formulate a plan to solve this horrendous problem. Bert would roundup the boys he used on his farm in Prince Albert, while I would do the same in Saskatoon. I would pick up the necessary equipment needed for the repair as Bert and his crew were driving the one hundred miles to Saskatoon from Prince Albert! We could expect to see them within two hours.

We shut the self waterers and feeders off and began catching birds that had gotten loose when their cage doors had sprung open. Bert thought we would have to cut the cages into10 foot lengths in order to lift them back into position, which meant renting four cum-a-longs (used for lifting loads) from an equipment rentals business. It took fourteen of us about nine hours to get those cages back up in the air, while the row of birds above us very excitedly went about the business of eating, drinking, and crapping on us below!! As the cages were cut into 10 foot lengths, the water lines and food augers were separated as well, then pieced back together as each section of cage was raised into position. It was a grueling and very unpleasant job, but it had to be done, and we couldn't quit until it was finished! We rested once during the whole nightmare, to stop for something to eat. It was about 10P.M. when we complete the repair and Bert was able to climb into his van and take his tired, dirty crew back to P.A.!

Being in business for yourself isn't everything it's cracked up to be! It isn't a 9 to 5 job and you can't leave the job at the office. A poultry farm is even more demanding because by it's very nature the animals producing the product we were marketing had to be properly sheltered, fed, watered and protected from disease. Agribusiness is risky at the best of times, with about the only guarantee being lots of hard work. Just getting those eggs to our tables in the morning is really a monumental task, requiring the efforts of many people. It seems odd that while agriculture is so very important to our existence, we, as a people have so distanced ourselves from it?

As we went about the day to day operation of the poultry farm it became apparent that we couldn't repair, replace or change everything screaming for attention for lack of sufficient funds. We had to prioritize each problem and attempt to solve them based on their importance, as finances allowed. We had a problem with moisture in our barns which Bert thought could best be resolved by improving ventilation. Archie Hugo, a carpenter who had done a lot of work for Bert, was dispatched to place a new baffle board system along with insulation in our worst barns. This would reduce excess moisture in our barns, reducing wire marks on our eggs and aid us in marketing a better product.This task alone took Archie the better part of a year and along with other jobs we had for him he more or less stayed at our farm throughout the week and went home to P.A. on the weekends. Carol cooked the meals and never complained, even though she wasn't compensated. She knew there were sacrifices we all had to make and she was prepared to do her part to help us succeed.

The chick barn was always a pleasure to work in because the chicks were so cute. We would get the day old chicks delivered (17,000 at a time) from our hatchery and place them in the freshly cleaned preheated barn one hundred to a cage. These cages were large enough to allow for future growth of the chicks and paper had been placed on the floors of the cages so their small feet wouldn't go through the spaces between the wire.At one week of age we set up the debeaking tables and each birds beak was cut to a set length to keep cannibalism to a minimum. We never lost more than ten chicks as a result of this procedure. At three weeks of age the combs of the cockerels missed during chick sexing were quite noticeable and they were removed from the flock with the exception of a dozen or so kept for crowing and making the hens feel good! Cockerels don't lay eggs. Finally after about eighteen weeks in the chick barns the young pullets would begin laying small eggs, a sign it was time to move to a layer barn where they would be brought into lay. The old flock would be moved out by semi truck to a kill plant, the barn thoroughly cleaned and disinfected and the new pullets moved into their new home for the next year. We grew two flocks of chicks on "Starline Farms" each year.

One very cold January morning as I was walking towards the barns two of the staff greeted me with the shocking news that the hens were dying in one of the barns! Upon entering the barn I found that the top level of birds had expired during the night but that the middle and lower levels were still alive!The temperature had dropped so much that only one of the huge fans had barely been turning. The moisture buildup had slowly frozen and the resulting ice had finally stopped the fan from running. As the oxygen level dropped from the ceiling down the birds started dying! I was in a state of shock! This had been the first flock of layers I had raised from chicks and I was watching them carefully to see what kind of egg production they would achieve. A great deal of work had gone into these birds and it was snuffed out when that one fan stopped working! We pulled 4500 dead birds out of the cages and removed them from the barn. There would be no egg production from this flock and of course we weren't going to make any money either!

Every mistake we made, increased our costs. We installed a feed mill with the idea of cutting feed costs several hundred dollars a day. However every little problem, such as incorrect proportioning of an ingredient, or perhaps running out of an ingredient, might take a few hours or perhaps even a few days to be noticed. Egg production and quality would be affected and once again, up went the costs! There are huge companies milling feed for poultry operations all over North America, and believe me, they have all kinds of breakdowns and problems every day! This is a separate business in and of itself. Sometimes I think we tried to do too much all at once! At the time I just didn't have the experience to make a good argument against implementing this procedure into "Starline Farms" operation. Besides, Bert was the majority shareholder and he wanted the feed mill! I just had to live with the thing and try to make it work!

Carol presented me with the gift of a second baby boy in April of 1979! We named him Mark and he was our only Saskatchewan baby. Mark would be great company for his older brother David in sixteen months or so and of course I couldn't help thinking that one day he would be helping me around the farm. Our little family wasn't so little anymore with two girls and two boys, all the bedrooms were full! It was a happy family though and the kids who remember those days on the farm feel the same. Of course they weren't involved with the business aspects of the whole operation but I'm talking about the family's quality of life.

Carol and I tried to take advantage of the space we had available on the farm with picnics, hikes and tobogganing whenever we had the chance. As we lived so close to

Saskatoon, Carol would take the kids to a lovely park with a pool on the warm summer days. This proximity to the big city really was a plus for our whole family, for shopping, and for entertainment. We could always take in a movie or go to a good restaurant if we felt the need.On Sundays we usually attended church in Saskatoon while the boys I had working for us gathered eggs. It seemed odd in a way that even when we were off the farm, shopping or visiting, there was always work going on at the farm.

A simple power failure could spell disaster on a poultry farm because the electrical systems required to supply the water, feed and provide cooling for the birds had to work twenty four/seven! This meant backup emergency power provided by a generator. We had a huge walk in freezer which we leased out. When the power failed, the freezer compressors shut down as the generator couldn't handle the load. When power returned the compressors had to be restarted manually or the freezer contents began to thaw out! Attention to detail often spelled the difference between a small accident becoming a major disaster. Even with the constant vigilance paid to testing and checking systems we still had many problems. Every manager of a large scale poultry operation such as ours could attest to the fact that no matter how carefully one tests the equipment failures still occur and accidents still happen.

In February of 1980,Carol and I, along with Ron and Danielle Fraser took a two week vacation to the Bahamas. The weather was great and we had fun doing the usual ; sightseeing, scuba diving, snorkeling, and dining.I was deeply disturbed by the poverty which we saw when we strayed from the advertised tourist haunts! Small wonder that many vendors of straw or wood crafts had drugs for sale under the counter! Everyone was trying to make a living and the profit potential of drugs was too tempting for many to resist. Ron being a policeman said he could have made more busts here in one day then he could have in a month back home!

The beaches on Paradise Island were patrolled and the island was separated from Nassau by a toll bridge. We had the most enjoyment from sunbathing and snorkeling just off the white sand beaches. There was a rumor that the exiled "Shaw of Iran" was staying in a beautiful home on Paradise Island, which we walked by each day on our way to the beach, however we never saw any hint of him if he was there. The two weeks came to an end and I was glad to climb on an Air Canada plane to head home! The stewardess kept me in the best tasting coffee I had ever had!

We arrived to the cold harsh reality of a Saskatchewan winter day. Arriving at the farm I was rapidly briefed by my father(who had been helping out in my absence) on everything that had gone amiss. A manure auger had been torn off one barn by accident! A motor had been blown out of our new 5 ton truck by accident! Everything else was fairly minor but I remember my dad's parting remarks as he prepared to head home to Quesnel, B.C. "Darwin, this business has **nothing going for it**"!

Gradually the feeling that things were not going well business wise began to nag me. Despite our best efforts after two years in business we were about $ 200,000.00 in the red! Our first year in business we had lost about $120,000.00 on a two point eight million gross; the second year we lost about $80,000.00 on a three point two million dollar gross! It was extremely difficult for me after earning sixteen thousand dollars gross in 1977, with the telephone company, to understand how on a six million dollar gross we couldn't make a dime? The " Bank" we had negotiated our quarter million dollar **line of credit** with had us come in (that's all four of the partners) and asked us collectively what was wrong and how could they help?!

The message was clear, the bank was watching us very closely and we had better start turning a profit very soon or they would call in their line of credit and force us out of business! I remember the ride up in the elevator to the tenth floor of the bank, walking directly into this huge office on a sumptuous carpet and sitting opposite this little god who would decide our fate. It seemed to me that we were really working for the bankers! I recall thinking that the most difficult work these guys did each day was to turn their computers on and decide who they wanted to turn the screws on today! I marvelled at the power of large companies, but the banks are very powerful as well. The illusion of democracy is that the people have the power! We may have a great deal of freedom in a democracy, but the real power is reserved for the organizations with money!

The saying " Power corrupts and absolute power corrupts absolutely" or " The love of money is the root of all evil" comes to mind whenever I think of the banking system. The banks seem to have a hidden agenda in this country and maybe it is to eventually own every thing here! If a banker loans you $100.00 at 10% simple interest payable in one year, then where does the interest come from to repay the bank loan at year end? I don't understand economics at all.

As I rode the elevator down I knew that something had changed! My attitude maybe, my thinking processes maybe, I'm not sure to this day, but I did get a real education in that banker's office! I discovered very quickly who the real boss was! Bert wasn't the boss nor were the partners who had the shares in the business, the banker was the boss; We could do anything we wanted as long as the bank said Yes!After the bank meeting the four of us had a meeting of our own and gradually reached the conclusion that we were more or less unhappy with the partnership as it stood. We decided to restructure and when it was over John Paley and Bob Schultz owned " Millar Hatcheries" and the Regina portion of "Star

Egg Company". Bert and I had "Starline Farms" and the Saskatoon portion of "Star Egg Company".

Carol and Bert were not getting along well, because she told him what she thought of the way he did things and he didn't like it! Bert had a habit of coming out to the farm several times a week after " Star Egg" closed for the day. He liked to stay for supper and the two of us would often play a game of chess after supper. I enjoyed this, but Carol wasn't happy about it. It was a hundred miles home each evening and sometimes Bert didn't feel like making that trip. This went on for awhile and finally one evening for whatever the reason Carol told Bert she thought he should be going home to his wife and kids in Prince Albert after work not coming to our place to play chess! Carol was right but neither Bert nor I for that matter cared to admit it at the time. However she made her point and from that moment on we saw a whole lot less of my brother in law!

One Sunday afternoon Bert called and wanted to talk to me. Carol told him she was cutting the girls hair, but if it was really important she would go to the barns where I was working and have me call Bert back. If it wasn't pressing business she was going to finish the girl's hair and then go down to the barns and find me. I don't know who was to blame but Bert said that maybe he should have the phone removed and hung up on Carol! That was really the kiss of death to the relationship between Carol and Bert! With all the problems we were having; the long hours of work and losing money on top of it all; Carol and I began to discuss returning to B.C.

"Starline Farms" was put up for sale and several buyers lined up to place offers. The first group was unsuccessful in their attempts to secure financing, but the second offer was accepted. "Starline Farms" was sold to Carol Teichroeb, a neighbor of ours whose son worked for me. If memory serves me correctly she was the president of the Canadian Turkey

Marketing Board, extremely capable and well connected! I remember hearing that she had only recently returned from China on a business trip with Eugene Whelan the Federal Minister of Agriculture. At any rate Mrs. Teichroeb's daughter and son in law wanted to get into the business and to get quota you had to buy a farm. "Starline Farms" was only a couple of miles away from the Teichroeb's farm and that fit right in with their plans. The sale completed, the Teichroeb's daughter and son in law started coming to the farm to familiarize themselves with day to day operation.

My wife and I determined that we would head for Kelowna, B.C. as her parents lived there and we had visited several times on holidays and really liked it. Kelowna was a retirement area and a highly desirable place to work and live because of it's climate and location in the Okanagan Valley. The problem was until I could get my money out of the company I was basically broke! I'm not exaggerating when I say that until the day before we left I never knew whether or not the bank was going to lend me the money to pay for the moving van! Isn't it strange how we make our requests known to that invisible God whenever we need something or are in deep trouble? I prayed as did Carol and a half hour before the close of the banking day on Friday, the bank called and gave their okay to the loan! We rejoiced to know we could pay for the rental truck and load up Saturday and leave for Kelowna on Sunday!

Our boys got us loaded up on Saturday and tearfully said goodbye as they gave us a set of matched towels(**one of which eventually ended up on Lee's woodpile**) to dry our eyes with! Having made arrangements with Greig Hamilton to keep an eye on the place, we left the farm and Saskatchewan, never to return. It was about 4:PM when I jumped behind the wheel of the U-Haul and headed for B.C. with Carol, and our four children following behind in the station wagon.

By 11P:M we were approaching the outskirts of Calgary and I was so tired that I just pulled over onto a side road, crawled into the rear of the station wagon and went to sleep. When we awoke the next morning the inside of the wagon's windows was covered with a type of frost caused by the vapor from our breath. We couldn't see a anything through the windows even though it was only mid August the cool air told me that winter wasn't far off! We warmed up the vehicles and drove on towards Banff, stopping at a restaurant along the way for breakfast. Then we were off on the second leg of our journey up into the Rockies.

While I was unsure about the future and what I would be doing for a living, we had previously rented a duplex in Westbank, and knew we had a place to live when we arrived. I was free of the farm and the responsibilities of the livestock, egg production, staffing, and any of the hundred other problems that arose each day! I was also excited at the prospects of returning to B.C. I was confident that I could find a job and provide for my family; I always had! To his credit, Bert had agreed to pay me my salary for the next six months, and eventually I should get some of my investment back. I would have work and be nicely settled in before my wages from "Starline Farms" ran out. All of these thoughts flooded my mind as we drove towards British Columbia.~

The Trial, Mistrial
and Aftermath

—⟋⟍—

April 15th, 1996 began as any other beautiful spring day with sun pouring in the window. I had been awake most of the night, but delayed getting dressed as if staying there would somehow delay the trial. Finally when I knew I could delay no longer, I rose and began dressing in the slacks and sports jacket I had chosen to wear. After choking down some toast and coffee, I headed to the bathroom to brush my teeth. There on the vanity was a note of inspiration from Carol, with a scripture reference.That note calmed me and in a strange almost nonchalant manner I left the house in my car and drove to the courthouse where Brian met me and escorted me to the courtroom. Once inside we approached the bench of this rather opulent room of light oak with beautiful red carpeting. The whole building was state of the art, having only recently been built.

Brian and his assistant, Michael Bain, had chairs and a desk located at the front of the courtroom. In front of them and at a higher level, were some staff including the court secretary. Higher still was the bench where the judge would sit. Three levels of gorgeous golden oak furniture on which the officers of the court would sit. To the right of defense counsel, sat Crown counsel. Adjacent to the bench were two rows of pews which sat the jury. I was seated in the docket, a glass enclosed box, on the left side of the courtroom, with a sheriff standing next to me. The whole area of the court was separated from the seating area by a beautifully finished oak fence running the width of the courtroom. The gallery was large, containing comfortable seating for the onlookers.

As I took my place in the docket, the courtroom filled, until the door leading to judge's chambers opened and the bailiff commanded " **All rise**"

Everyone present stood and the procedure began.The judge responded that everyone sit, and called for me to rise as he read the charges against me. At the quiet coaching of my lawyer standing next to me, I pled not guilty to all charges, when asked, and we moved on to the lengthy process of choosing the jury. There were approximately one hundred people who had been summoned from which the jury of twelve would be chosen.

Each legal team had it's criteria for the selections they made and of course their choices were subject to the challenges of the other side. This process took a day and a half to complete, after which the judge adjourned for lunch. Upon reconvening after lunch the judge began by reading a note given him by the jury foreman.The note, written by a juror, informed the judge she couldn't render an impartial decision. She was the mother in law of my co-worker and friend, **Fred Bellis's daughter!** At this revelation the judge responded to the court that he felt he had no other option than to call a **Mistrial!**

The judge said an attempt to recall the people from which the jury had been chosen to get another juror would be made but he wasn't optimistic as the legal teams had already exhausted their challenges! The trial ended abruptly with everyone shocked as we all rose and the judge exited the courtroom! I was informed by Brian, **that this delay had just cost me ten thousand dollars!** (mentioned earlier) It wasn't his fault, as the scheduling for his whole law practice would have to be changed as a new trial date would have to be set. What a completely unforeseen change of events this had become. Eventually a new trial date of July 08, 1996 was set so let's get right to it as we were all prepared for it, right?

We're back in the courtroom, Monday, July 08; a new jury in place, and our ace legal team satisfied with it's selection. **A decision allowing audio tapes of my interrogation in January of 1995, by the R.C.M.P. has been made in our favor.** I was informed that three churches were praying for me.... " **The effectual fervent prayer of a righteous man availed much!"**

Just moments before the judge was due to enter the courtroom a deputy with the sheriff's department approached Michael Bain and myself while we were standing and talking at the defense desk and said to me, "Sir, we're about ready to begin here, would you have your client enter the docket please?" We all had a good laugh over that, as the deputy had mistaken me for the lawyer, and Michael for the client! I entered the docket, where I would be under constant scrutiny for the duration of the trial. I was extremely uneasy as I wondered what kind of signals I would be sending out with my body language. As I listened to Judge Hamilton instructing the jury that I was innocent until proven guilty; that I need not say anything to defend myself; that it was up to the Crown to prove my guilt..... I couldn't help but ask myself the question why was it costing me everything to hire the best legal help I could get? Why didn't the state pay for this trial or any trial until a person was in fact found guilty? Even if I were by some chance to be found innocent, it was going to cost me everything I had!

Mr. Schlosser, the Crown Counsel began by outlining the case against me and presenting the undisputed facts of the shooting incident. Evidence provided by the police present that evening was introduced to the Court throughout the first and second days of the trial, supplemented by the evidence of the attending physician, who had stitched Lee up and removed some of the pellets. The paramedics testified, as did my son Mark, and Dianne Roth(as hostile witnesses) which completed the second day of testimony.

Wednesday, July10th and Day 3 - Things really started to get interesting for me as this was the day that Stephen Lee was to testify. Gavin Gibb, Lee's friend, testified just before Lee was called and his testimony was unremarkable. My goal here is to provide the reader with a feeling of how things went during the trial, covering the interesting parts in some detail while glossing over the more mundane less interesting stuff. Having said that I'll move right to Lee's testimony and begin with some of the cross examination testimony.

Q. Mr. Lee, you were shot by a man who has eight children and has been working for 25years,and put everything in his life at risk. Why do you think he did that?

A. Cause Mr. uh Mr. Demers came out and did what he did to me because we had a fist fight and he came out to beat me up and he had not had that chance to do that, he got the worst of it, and just on the threats after that fight, I put that together why he did what he did.

Q. Okay

A. He was gonna get even with me, and he did.

Q. Do you recall saying sir, when you were in the hospital to the nurses, I guess I pushed him too far?

A. No, I didn't say that, Your Honour.

Q. Did you say anything of that nature?

A. No, I never, Your Honour.

Q.Was it true? Did you push him too far?

A. I never dealt with the man, Your Honour.

Q. Well, this incident that you talked about with the fight, it didn't quite happen the way you've said, did it? You went.... You testified that you just went over there with the fingers to come outside, right?'

A. I did say— I did do that, Your Honour.

Q. Okay, Well, if it was involved with David, why did you do that? Why didn't you stop at the door and say to Mr. Demers, I'd like to talk about your son, David?

A. Cause Your Honour, I explained to Mr. Demers in October the situation with my dad dying and I don't want no antagonizement, and when I found out that he put those trees on the border line without even asking me and having his kid, David, put them there, taking gouges out of my property, then that upset me.

A. I'm sorry, I thought the fight was over David throwing rocks on your roof?

A. That was part of the harassment that I was gonna go over there to talk to him about.

Q. Oh, so the incident wasn't about David throwing rocks on the roof, it was about trees, was it?

A. No, it wasn't, Your Honour, it was also about David throwing rocks at my residence.

Q. I see, Well, you see, you told the police in your statement that you went over there and the first thing you did was look at him and he was in the kitchen and went, You're an asshole.

A. I did say that, Your Honor.

Q. Well, is that the way you dealt with things generally in the couple of years, you and Mr. Demers?

A. That's the only time I ever spoke with Mr. Demers.

Q. So the first time you talked to him you said, You're an Asshole?

A. I looked at him and I pointed for him to come out and says, You are an Asshole. I did say that, Your Honour.

Q. So that was your introduction to Mr. Demers, was it, calling him an asshole?

A. It was, knowing that he knew the situation that I was dealing with.

Q. I see, Tell me, have you— did you have any troubles with other I neighbours?

A. Your Honour, I never had a problem with any of the neighbours until Mr. Demers and me had a fight.

Q. And then, you had other problems with neighbours then, did you?

A. They were dragged into it.

Q. How were they dragged into it?

A. I had a chat with the neighbour two doors from me, uh, about a month and a half after the fight and I had a problem with his nephew which was hanging around with Mr. Demers second oldest son, Mark. I was coming up the road in my vehicle with my son and they were being very sarcastic to me. My —my window was down and I heard them. I stopped and told them, I says, Is there a reason for you guys to be sarcastic to me? And they got very mouthy, so I went and talked with Don, which was the neighbour two doors from me. I told him, why is your— I didn't even know this kid was the nephew to begin with,he told me, uh, but I knew he lived there. I says, This kid here is harassing me with Mark. And Don Harvey says, Yeah, he says , I've heard about you, He says, Why don't you pick on somebody your own size? He says, uh, You went and picked a fight with Mr. Demers, and I said, Don, I says, how would you know that? I've never told you about the situation. So he was, uh basically filled in of what the Demers family wanted that family to know.

Q. I see, Tell me, this incident with Mark and — was it Mark, did you say?

A. Yes it was, Your Honour.

Q. And Don Harvey's nephew, Jeff?

A. Yes, Your Honour.

Q. And what were they doing?

A. They were, — I was driving by with my son, I'd just come back from the mailbox, and , uh, as I was driving by they were.... So I stopped and says, you know, There's no reason to be like that with to me. I don't even know this kid.

Q. That's Mr. Harvey, is it?

A. Don Harvey's nephew, yes Your Honour.

Q. And during this conversation, did you refer to the Demers?

A. I may have, Your Honour.

Q. As a matter of fact, sir, I'm suggesting to you that you said, Even if they move,— I'm going to go after them even if they move.Do you recall saying that ?

A. Definitely did not say that, Your Honour.

Q. Did you tell Mr. Harvey that you had a gun and that you had ways to get back at him?

A. No, Your Honour.

Q. Nothing of that nature?

A. No, Your Honour.

Q. Have you ever said anything of that nature to anybody in this neighbourhood?

A. No, Your Honour.

Q. Did you say the Demers can run, but they can't hide?

A. No, Your Honour.

Q. How about, I've got ways to deal with people like that?

A. No, Your Honour.

Q. Tell me, when you were in the hospital, did you make threats against the Demers to the nurses?

A. I was very upset for what had happened to me, I may have said something. I don't remember.

Q. How about something like, hey what Demers can do in three shots I can do with one? Do you remember saying something like that?

A. I don't remember.

Q. Do you remember an incident in the hospital where the fellow across the bed from you was beaten up? He was saying he was beaten up and you said, All you gotta do is phone me and I'll take care of it?

A. I didn't say that, Your Honour.

Q. That didn't happen, did it?

A. No, Your Honour.

Q. That's not something you would say then?

A. No, Your Honour.

Q. Never?

A. Never, Your Honour.

Q. How about, did you tell Mr. Harvey you were a karate expert?

A. No, Your Honour.

Q. Did you tell Mr. Harvey, hey I go out at night and you never know what I do at night?

A. No, Your Honour.

Q. You phoned more people than the police,didn't you? Did you phone the fire department?

A. I did, Your Honour... I saw smoke coming from the side of his house, Your Honour.

Q. And did he?

A. From when the fire chief come,he said there was no burning barrel there.

Q. Yeah, in fact, it was smoke coming from the Demers chimney, wasn't it?

A. That's what it appeared to be, Your Honour, yeah.

Q. Was there an incident where you saw— you knew that Mr. Demers worked for B. C. Tel.?

A. Yes, Your Honour.

Q. Did you phone B. C. Tel and say Hey, I think you've got a guy here who's taking time off work and is at home right now, because you saw his truck?

A. I never did it myself, Your Honour.

Q. Oh, You know about it though. Do You?

A. Uh, I know, — yes, I do.

Q. Who did that, then?

A. It was a friend, Your Honour.

Q. A friend at your house?

A. :Yes, Your Honour.

Q. I see, and phoned three times?

A. I'm not sure how many times, Your Honour.

Q. And I'm sorry, It turned out it wasn't Mr. Demers at all because Mr. Demers was down at the coast (**note: Playing Chess in the Paul Keres Memorial Chess Tournament - a 3 day tournament with John Nuefeld his realtor and friend who later sold the Demers home) (Lee had mistaken another employee's company vehicle as mine)**

A. Your Honour, Mr. Demers was seen leaving that vehicle sitting there for an hour and a half on a statutory holiday in the home.

Q. Oh, he was was he?

A. Yes, Your Honour.

Q. Tell me, how did that occur that the friend would phone B.C. Tel.?

A. Because he doesn't believe that, uh, paying for that sort of business, that a man should be sitting at home being paid double or triple time on a statutory holiday.

Q. M' hmm. who's the friend?

A. Robby Frazer.

Q. Was he a neighbour?

A. No, Your Honour.

Q. So, he's got nothing to do with Mr. Demers or knows Mr. Demers?

A. No, Your Honour

Q. I take it he called in after you talked to him though?

A. He's well aware of our problems that we had with the children— or the child

Q. So, I'm fair in saying then that the reason that B.C. Tel. was called, was you believed Mr. Demers was there and you wanted to get Mr. Demers in trouble, fair enough?
A. Didn't wanna get Mr. Demers in trouble.
Q. You didn't ?
A. No, Your Honour.
Q. Well, what did you think— if it was Mr. Demers there, what did you think the ramifications were going to be?
A. Well, I figure if — I'm just like anybody, If you're gonna be given a pay cheque, work for your money—
Q. Right
A. Not th— not sit there an hour and a half being paid double time or triple time. I'n not sure what it was, but, it was a statutory holiday.
Q. Well—
A. and I think somebody should report that , whether, it was just— whether it was just Mr. Demers or anybody.
Q. I see. So you're saying that if the next door neighbour was like your best friend you'd still do the same thing?
A. I would at least talk to him.
Q. Did you report Mr. Demers for having a basement suite?
A. No, Your Honour.
Q. Did you ever tell David Demers that you were going to crush his head with a rock and put him in a coma for two weeks?
A. No, I never, Your Honour.
Q. You've never said anything like that to any of those guys?
A. I never did, Your Honour.
Q. Did you ever— do you know the lady who lives in the basement of the Demers suite?
A. I don't know her personally, but I know of her.
Q. And correct me if I'm wrong, that she and Mrs. Demers used to go for walks often.

A. Yes Your Honour.

Q. And you would follow them?

A. No, Your Honour.

Q. You wouldn't follow them?

A. No, Your Honour

Q. Were you ever in the vicinity when they were walking?

A. I was always in my yard when I did see them.

Q. Did you ever talk to the neighbours about the Demers?

A. I have talked to a few of the neighbours about the problems I was having

Q. I understand in this incident where you talked about the kids making fun of you, Jeff and Mark, that you said you were going to rip their heads off and shove it up their ass?

A. No, Your Honour.

Q. That didn't occur either?

A. No, Your Honour. I asked Don Harvey if he would take care of his cousin when I found out— or his nephew. I says, Will you take care of him please?

Q. That's all you said?

A. That's all I said, Your Honour.

Q. Tell me did you ever use foul language around these people at all?

A. No, uh, I never used foul language, Your Honour.

Q. Never?

A. Never!

Q. Do you recall after the window incident that you thought that David had broken your window?

A. David did break my window, Your Honour.

Q. Did you see him break it?

A. I never saw him break it, Your Honour

Q. So you assumed he broke it?

A. I assumed he broke it because he threw seven rocks while I was standing there.

Q. Seven?

A. Seven rocks, Your Honour.

Q. You counted them? Seven?

A. I picked them all up off the ground.

Q. This is when he was mowing the lawn?

A. And I, uh, asked him to stop and he kept doing it.

Q. Did you tell Mrs. Demers that — you talked to Mrs. Demers after that didn't you?

A. No, I never Your Honour.

Q. Didn' t you tell her you would have her job at the school?

A. I knew Mrs. Demers was a noon hour supervisor. I did.

Q. And did you tell her you were going to have her job?

A. No, I never, Your Honour. What I told Mrs. Demers was, My kids go to the school. Whatever problems we have, don't take it out on my kids.

Q. Oh, so you didn't say anything about you're going to - I'm going to make sure you lose your job?

A. No, Your Honour.

Q. When the Demers would be out on their patio would you just go out and stare them down?

A. No, Your Honour.

Q. Tell me, out of all the incidents you've described them as numerous were any of these incidents your fault?

A. Your Honour, I'm not a perfect person.

Q. All right, and for instance, I was thinking about when you went over to Mr. Demers and called him a fucking asshole.

A. I never called him a fucking asshole, Your Honour.'

Q. Oh, I'm sorry, an asshole then?

A. Yes, Your Honour.

Q. You're telling this court, that Mrs. Demers, the mother of eight children, gave you the finger?

A. Sure did, Your Honour.

Q. And you,— were with Mr. Gibb at the time?

A. Yes, I was, Your Honour.

Q. Okay, Did you say anything to him? Hey that woman's giving me the finger, or whatever? Did you say anything?

A. Can't remember, Your Honour.

Q. But did he know about it?

A. Can't remember, Your Honour.

Q. You gave her the finger?

A. I returned one back, Your Honour.

Q. I was just wondering, remember giving a statement that evening?

A. That evening?

Q. Sorry, the next day, to the police.

A. Yes.

Q. All right, you said, " She was laughing at me, and, uh, I'm **not sure, whether she gave me the finger,** but I'm pretty sure she did, cause I retaliated. I went " **Fuck You"**.

A. Your Honour, I just got finished being operated on. I was coming out of anesthetic. I don't really— there's a lot of things in there that I said that, uh, didn't make sense.

Q. Oh, I see. Well, that wouldn't make sense, but it's a question of whether it's true or not?

A. Mrs. Demers gave me the finger, Your Honour.

Q. That's despite the fact the next day you couldn't recall whether she did or not?

A. Your Honour, there was,— I wasn't even making sense when I read that, I — it didn't make sense to me. I just vaguely remember talking to the officer.

Q. You said yesterday, I know exactly what I said. I said, "Happy New Year"

A. I said, Happy New Year with a wave.

Q. And in the statement you said you said, Merry Christmas.

A. In the statement I did say, " Merry Christmas" I didn't say that.

Q. As I say, it's a minor point, but I was wondering, when did you realize that the statements were different?

A. When I first got to look at my statements.

Q. What other things were there in the statements that were inaccurate?

A. I'd have to go through them again.

Q. Well, when you said to the police that you gave the finger and went fuck you, did you say, " Fuck You"?

A. Don't recall, Your Honour.

Q. Here's a woman, you gave her the finger, surely you recall wheather Mr. Gibb, who was there, knew about it or not. Did you say something like, That bitch?

A. Never said that bitch, Your Honour.

Q. Oh, I know that, but what did you say, if anything?

A. I can't recall.

Q. I put it to you that you said certain things in the hospital that you deny, but I understand that after the police talked to the nurses they came to you and asked you to surrender your guns. Do you recall that?

A. Yes, Your Honour.

Q. And you did so?

A. I did, Your Honour.

Q. And how many guns did you have?

A. I have six guns, Your Honour.

Q. Did you tell the nurse in the hospital you had nine?

A. No, Your Honour.

Q. I understand you used to walk up and down the street and go into the bushes carrying your gun.

A. Your Honour, what I used to do is take my gun from my home and walk right into the bush, yes, Your Honour.

Q. And that would happen often, wouldn't it?

A. It would only happen in hunting season.

Q. Did you ever tell, for instance the Harveys that you were an expert marksman?

A. Never, Your Honour, cause I'm not.

Q. Tell me, these people, the Harvey's and the neighbours, I put certain suggestions to you as what I termed as threats to the Demers, is this the reason if — that you can think of why they would say these things if they're not true?

A. Yes, Your Honour.

Q. Okay, what's the reason?

A. I don't know these are the exact reasons, but, uh, the Harveys understand the situation with this case. They know it's a very serious case. They are willing to, uh, get involved. Some of the statements that they have made are— uh, for a religious people, they're very, very, very, cruel statements, and they're willing to, uh, bend backwards to get Mr. Demers out of the trouble that he's in. They even went as far as putting tripods and cameras on me. I have been totally antagonized since this has happened from this family. What they've been basically trying to do is get— do something to me so that I'll retaliate so that they can say, see, told you this is the type of guy that I am, which I'm not that type of guy. I have been labelled a very vicious person, and this is why the actions was taken that Mr. Demers had done to me.

Q. Except for a couple of things, Mr. Lee. Number One, it was the Harveys that moved out of the neighborhood, right?

A. The Harveys moved out of the neighborhood and we— I knew why they moved out of the neighborhood. To put this case together...

Q. Oh, I see, it wasn't because of you harassing them and threatening them?

A. No, Your Honour.

Q. And Mr. Demers put his house up for sale in September of last year?

A. Yes, Your Honour.

A. For one thing, Your Honour, uh, I'm not sure why, but I do know we have a highway coming through and it's going right past their home.

Q. You know very well the reason they put up their house for sale is to get away from you, Mr. Lee.You know that, don't you?————

A. No, Your Honour.

Q. All, right, You know the woman in the basement?

A. I do, Your Honour.

Q. Did you yell to her one day, "You're gonna be sleeping with one eye open?"

A. No, never, Your Honour.

Q. Okay.

A. Mrs. Diane Roth never had anything to do with this.

Q. No? Did you tell the kids you were going to shoot their fucking old man?

A. Never, Your Honour.

Q. And I'm not just talking about their kids, but the kids in the neighborhood, that accompanied them.

A. Never once said that, Your Honour. We had a fist fight, me and Mr. Demers, and that's where it stood. We knew where we stood. That's why we never talked after that.

Q. Now your testimony— I want to get this clear. Your testimony is while the police officer is standing there that Mr. Demers made threats against you?

A. The officers were there when he threatened me.

Q. I understand— talking about the policeman when the window incident happened, you didn't know it was David, you assumed it was— but the crack in the window was barely visible?

A. Yes, Your Honour.

Q. But, you thought it was significant enough to phone the police?

A. See, Your Honour, to begin with, we never ph— I never phoned the police for the crack in the window. The rocks were thrown as it was getting dark. We had just come out of — off the lake and we were having a barbeque and we heard these noises. So I went and looked off my balcony and there was David cutting the grass, throwing these rocks, while the lawnmower was still running, at my home. So that's fine. I went out in the front and I asked David, " Don't throw rocks at my house." And he kept throwing them. So that's fine. I got hold of the police. I picked up the rocks for the evidence. I never noticed the window was broke until the next morning. The officer hadn't even come yet. It was dark. I never saw it, because it was right in the corner of the window, until the next morning.

Q. And can you describe your attitude towards the police on that occasion?

A. On that occasion, Your Honour, I was, uh, a little bit perturbed for the simple fact that I was a complaintiff and the officers never showed up that evening, and when they did show up— they did come to my house, but I was not home, but they went and they talked to the person I was complaining against, got the full statement, and then, when the officer came to my house to talk to me, his first words to me was he's heard enough, he's had enough of what he's heard. And then that's when I said to him, I says, Do you know these people?" And I also said to him, I know what's happening here. I says, Will you please get off my property? I says I don't want to discuss this any more. And he says to me, " You are a bully." and I says, " How would you know that?" I says, " That's something Mrs. Demers would say. How can you analyze me in a few minutes?" And I also told the officer, " I want your badge number and I want to talk to somebody over your head." He gave me the badge number, so I phoned the watchman and complained about how this matter was dealt with."

Q. You also told him you were going to take matters into your own hands.

A. I'm not sure exactly what I said to him, Your Honour.

Q. What did you mean by that?

A. I don't even remember saying that, Your Honour.

Q. Well, when you think back now, do you recall saying something of that nature?

A. I don't remember, Your Honour.

Q. As far as being a bully, that just twigged something on me. At Mr. Demers bail hearing the prosecutor described you as the neighbourhood bully.

A. Yes, Your Honour.

Q. Tell me in the past, sir where did you move to Westbank from?

A. I moved from Delta.

Q. Did you ever have any trouble with your neighbours in Delta?

A. Got along great with the neighbours.

Q. So you had no problems in the past with the neighbours?

A. Never.

Q. This is the first time?

A. It's the first time I've ever had a problem with, uh, some — — uh, you know, a problem like this.

Q. Well, not many people have problems like this, sir, but did you have problems in the past with neighbours?

A. No, Your Honour.

Q. Never?

A. Never, Your Honour.

Note: This testimony was in stark contrast to the private investigator, (a retired R.C. M. P. officer) who canvassed the neighbourhood in Delta where the Lee family had resided.! Without exception the neighbours who confided in the investigator, stated they were happy to see Steven Lee leave their area. Generally they said he was a foul mouthed bully of women and children, always causing trouble in the Delta neighbourhood.

Q. You also phoned the police because some bush was pulled up or something?

A. The bush was, uh, ripped right out of — just ripped right out and thrown right on the road.

Q. Did you see it happen?

A. I never saw it happen. No, I didn't , Your Honour.

Q. All right, So you didn't see it happen, you don't know who did it, but you phoned the police on the Demers?

A. Yes, Your Honour.

Q. Why did you do that?

A. To tell them the sort of problems that I've been having and this is starting to come to property being damaged.

Q. I see.

A. You gotta remember, we're on a dead end road and we don't have kids comin' up and down that road. We don't even have ' em trick or treater on that road.

Q. What made you think it was kids anyway?

A. Most kids do things like that, not adults, not mature adults.

Q. Okay, so the fact of the matter is you called the police having absolutely no evidence.

A. No evidence.

Q. And what was the purpose when you phoned them?

A. My purpose was to tell them that my property is being damaged. And it was basically to report it and, uh, this is the beginning of a new trend.

There is more, but I really wanted to give the reader an idea of the questions Mr. Lee was asked in cross examination by Mr. Jackson. **After the trial Stephen Lee told the news media that he felt as if he was the person on trial.** I believe he felt that way because the questions made him extremely uncomfortable, as many of the answers were half truths and some outright lies!

Steven Lee was followed on the stand by his daughter, Sheila, and his mother.... both contributed little of interest to the reader. Shiela, found it difficult to testify, as she was young and really liked my wife. I have no idea why she was made to testify?

When Shelley Lee, Steve's wife took the stand she reiterated virtually everything she had more or less been coached to say. There were no surprises to anyone in the courtroom until the cross examination began. Mr. Jackson's questions began innocently enough until he began to question her about her husband's temper and the language he used. As previously mentioned she stated he never used foul language and always got along with the neighbours.

Brian then asked her about Delta and how she got along with Steve. She replied well and then ever so quietly Brian said yes but you and the kids had to escape to a women's shelter when you were living in Delta, did you not? To which she replied, "Yes". Then Brian asked innocently, "What was that about?"

Shelley replied nervously, " I don't remember." which Brian followed with "Wasn't there something about sexual abuse?"

The judge slammed his gavel on the bench and immediately had the jury removed. He then demanded of Mr. Jackson what relevance these questions had to this case . He went on to state he knew what my lawyer was trying to do, (implying an assassination of Mr. Lee's character). Judge Hamilton chided Mr. Jackson for using this tactic and threatened him with contempt charges! Judge Hamilton then recalled the jury and instructed them to disregard the questions dealing with sexual abuse.

It was too late however, the damage had been done, from that moment on Steven Lee became the most mistrusted and disliked person in that courtroom!

Nobody believed Mrs. Lee's testimony after Brian was finished. It didn't even matter if it was true or not.... She couldn't be trusted and neither could her husband. The Lee's turned out to be their own worst enemies. As Mr. Jackson finished his questions and Shelley Lee was excused, you could have heard a pin drop in that courtroom. Everyone sat there in stunned silence until the Judge adjourned the proceedings for a brief break.

I was as stunned as everyone else present, as no one had told me anything about this. I did know that my lawyer had hired a private investigator to nose around down in the Lee's old neighbourhood in Delta, but I was not privy to any of the actual information he had brought to Brian. I guess Mr. Jackson had his own way of introducing evidence and didn't want to take any chances that the other side would find out what he had so they could prepare for some kind of rebuttal when it was introduced. I think Brian was also pretty sure he knew what the judge's reaction was going to be, so he kept it all to himself! It was blockbuster theatre however; very dramatic!

The last two people to testify that day were Sgt. Tidsbury of the R.C.M.P. (who had interrogated me the evening of the shooting) followed by Dr. Semrau (psychiatrist and expert witness for the Crown) who had also questioned me the evening I was incarcerated.

Their testimony that day was factual in that it dealt with the events of that evening when I was taken into custody, and the actual questions they asked that night and the answers that I gave. Nothing really sensational or exciting came out at this time but the next day the taped interviews were due to be heard in court— and I was extremely nervous about how they would sound to the jury?!

Day 4- July 11th, This was the day the Crown had determined to introduce the audio tapes made by the R.C.M.P. of my actual interrogation the night of the shooting. My defense team had proposed this evidence be heard by the jury and the judge had decided in favour of the defense. His reasons included that the audio tapes would accurately reflect my mental condition following the shooting just after my arrest.

Since the whole argument of the defense was my mental state at the time and just what had led up to this terrible event, it was thought to be one tool which should be made available to the jury in reaching their decision.

I was very nervous about listening to the tapes as I had no idea what their effect would be on the jury. The tapes were played to all present in the courtroom and while I tried to watch the jury for some telltale sign as to what they were thinking, I found myself becoming so immersed in the emotions of that evenings events I actually forgot about watching the jury. I became quite emotional as I listened to myself crying on the tapes and pouring my heart out to the R.C.M.P. interrogator, Sargeant. Tidsbury.

Later I was told that Stephen Lee, sitting in the gallery of the courtroom with his brother, (as he had finished giving all his evidence) was having quite a laugh at my apparent difficulties while they listened to the tapes.

Two more witnesses were called by the Crown that day. Mr. Mc Conachee, - a ballistics expert from the R.C.M.P. and Dr. Semrau the psychiatrist, both giving their expert opinions on Crown evidence. Mr. Schlosser, the Crown Counsel, then made a short summation of the evidence presented to date and ended by saying this concluded the Crown's evidence against me.

Just before leaving, Brian had me sit in a small conference room with him and informed me of an offer the Crown had made, which would involve me pleading guilty to a lesser charge and getting three years for same. I asked him what he thought we should do and he responded no way. However he was duty bound to present the offer to me. His opinion was that we hadn't presented our defense yet and he thought we had a good case. I agreed with him and we decided to go for broke. Next week the Court would finally hear our side of things!

Day 05-July 12th, began the first day of the defense's presentation of evidence and we opened with our character witnesses which included the testimony of both families who had lived next door (12 years) in the Lee house. Some of our witnesses were people who had worked with me and known me from as far back as the sixties. Of course without exception they all had glowing stories to relate to the Court concerning my sterling character! (They were credible witnesses)

Day 06- July15[th], saw the defense calling it's first real witness, Sheila Ferguson, a nurse who while attending Mr. Lee in the hospital, became quite concerned over some of the things he had been saying, and contacted the police. She was concerned that he was bragging to her and others that what I had failed to do to him with three shots he would do in one! She was so disturbed by his remarks and threats while there that in spite of her professionalism she become quite fearful of the man!

Our son David was called after Sheila, and he gave a fairly good account of his history with Stephen Lee which appeared to be honest and truthful. **Note: It was reported to me later, from fairly reliable sources that Stephen Lee was making threatening gestures with his fists towards David from where he was watching in the gallery and that several of the jury members were in fact watching him as he did it!**

Calvin Duchesne, married to our oldest daughter Karyn, and father of four daughters of his own was called by the Defense. His testimony dealt with not only the outrageous behavior of Lee witnessed by the Duchesne family when they visited our home, but the ongoing behavior of Stephen Lee after the shooting. Aside from the obvious support Calvin provided our testimony, it was his own personal experiences with Lee which added so much more evidence for the jury to consider.

One such piece of evidence presented by Calvin had taken place when he had come over to help Carol do some packing and moving of large boxes. As Calvin was leaving our home Lee had come driving up the road and seeing who it was had intentionally tried to run Calvin right off the road! Carol contacted me as I had to stay out of Westbank, (part of my bail conditions) and all I could suggest was that Calvin contact Brian, in Vancouver.

This Carol did and Brian advised her to have Calvin launch a complaint with the police. The reader would be aided to know the character of the fine man (Calvin) who married my daughter Karyn, to better understand his history of going out of his way to help others, his non violent nature, and his Christian personality to understand how difficult this whole affair became for him!

When Calvin finally went to testify against Lee in traffic court he found himself ,his wife and children physically threatened by Lee outside the courtroom after Lee lost the case and was fined!

This wasn't the end of it however, as after he got home he became so concerned with the threats he received from Lee concerning Karyn and their girls that he called Carol (now living on Dilworth Mt. in Kelowna) and related the events of what had just happened to him after Lee lost the traffic case in court   ! Once again Carol called Brian, who again instructed her to tell Calvin to contact the police and report what had happened. This was done, quite fortunately for Calvin, as it later turned out!

The next day as Calvin was having a shower the R.C. M. P. arrived at the Duchesne's door, and over Karyn's protestations walked into the bedroom, arrested Calvin, cuffed him and took him down to the Kelowna detachment!?!

Calvin was informed that a complaint had been sworn against him by Stephen Lee that Calvin had threatened him with assault to do bodily harm! While Calvin was flabbergasted at what was happening he informed the officer about Lee's loss in traffic court the day before and that it was Lee who had threatened Calvin and the whole Duchesne family, with threats of being shot! When asked if he could prove these serious accusations Calvin related that on the advice of the Demers family's lawyer he had reported the whole incident to the Westbank detachment of the R.C.M.P.

The officer was quite surprised to find that Calvin was telling the truth about the whole matter. Calvin then went on to relate that if the officer checked with the security department at the Kelowna Courthouse that Lee's threats should have been recorded by the security department's video tapes! This would have been wonderful evidence substantiating Calvin's assertions making his arguments overwhelming! When the tapes were checked it was determined that they are erased every 24hours?! (Why I don't know?)

Later when Calvin and Lee met in Court before a Judge in this matter, they were both granted restraining orders to stay away from each other's homes and in fact each other. Were either of them to break the restraining order they would have forfeited five thousand dollars. Calvin said he never saw hide nor hair of Steven Lee for a year after that restraining order was issued! Lee wasn't happy with the order either as he complained bitterly to the judge that he mowed lawns in Calvin's neighbourhood. The judge simply stated that if it was required of Calvin to stay away from the Lee residence, it was only fair to require a similar order from Lee!

Does the reader start to get the feeling the jury was getting about Stephen Lee? Why he was called the neighbourhood bully? Why he became impossible to believe? It gradually became a common belief that the guy was a compulsive liar, causing him to complain to the media that he felt he was on trial! In actuality I think the jury had already made up it's collective mind about Stephen Lee.... It was me they hadn't come to a conclusion about?!

Day 07- July 16th, Judy and Don Harvey, neighbours down the road from us were called next. Their testimony corroborated ours although it was overlapping, personalized, (their own personal experiences with Lee) and included many details not previously heard by the Court.

The Harveys, our neighbours, were a Christian family, and though friendly whenever they saw us, really hadn't become our friends as yet. Our children were classmates at school and did play together after school. I for example had only once been to the Harvey home and that was on New Years Evening, Jan.01, 95 - the day before the shooting. Carol and Judy Harvey did visit when they met one another shopping or on walks, or at school, but to my knowledge while on friendly terms, didn't visit back and forth. This eventually changed, as Carol and Judy became very good friends.

To the Harvey's credit they both testified truthfully to their actual experiences with Steven Lee. They risked the wrath of the man who was terrorizing our family turning his attentions on them. It didn't take Lee long to try some of his tactics on them either. Ultimately the Harvey family who had spent a great deal of time and money renovating their home were forced to sell and move just to get away from Steven Lee!

They had a lovely home with a gorgeous swimming pool and had no intention of leaving. Somehow when your life is turned into a nightmare, nothing seems worth the hell you're being put through just to live in a certain place! The Harvey's reluctantly put their home up for sale, just as we had before them, to get away from Lee!

When Judy and Don Harvey were finished testifying there was little doubt left in the minds of the jury as to the character of the man called Steven Lee! The Harvey children had been bullied, (as had our kids) while Mrs. Harvey had on several occasions heard Lee cursing and swearing. Judy had also watched Lee as he would follow Carol and Dianne when they went on their walks around the neighbourhood.

Even though Lee never wanted witnesses to his erratic behavior often his temper and foul mouth got the best of him as he blew his top and spewed forth a vicious diatribe at an unsuspecting victim. His tactics were made known to the whole courtroom much to his chagrin.

Carol followed the Harveys to the stand, which I was extremely nervous about. Here was my life partner, the mother of our eight children, who had been put through hell, lost her lovely home as a result of my reaction, now through no actions of hers having to testify in court! I couldn't bear listening to her...... yet somehow I had to ..... I had to pretend to be brave for her...... be calm ..... Present the right countenance before her thereby inspiring her to be relaxed as she told her story to the court!

It wasn't going to be like that though, nope not at all, I had trouble restraining my emotions which I'm sure she picked up on immediately! Carol was having trouble speaking as if she had a frog in her throat and she had to keep repeating herself, frequently stopping for a drink of water from the glass placed there for her convenience. Carol was understandably nervous made worse by the constant glare coming from Steven Lee!

I think the reasons why she was so uptight and nervous on the stand simply echoed how deeply Carol had been affected by this whole affair. The profound impact on her life was evident in every sentence she tried to speak. Her whole time on the stand was as agonizing for me as it no doubt was for her. Frankly I was relieved when she was excused from the stand.

Our second oldest daughter, Janice, was called to the stand next. She had looked after her brothers and sisters on several occasions in our absence and had a couple of experiences with Steven Lee and his dog the court were told about.

While her testimony about Lee was anything but flattering, it was more or less what one would expect to hear from a daughter trying to influence the court in her father's favour so I'll say little more about it. This completed day seven more or less and we adjurned for the day. Tomorrow promised to be exciting as the expert witnesses for the defense were due to be called!

July17th, 1996- Day08, **Expert Witnesses for the Defense**

Dr.S. Lohrasbe- Brief Curriculum Vitae

Forensic Psychiatric Experience:

Sessional employment since 1985 with the Forensic Psychiatric Services Commission. Between 1985 and September 1992, worked at the Forensic Psychiatric Institute in Port Coquitlam, providing assessment and treatment to the mentally disordered. Since September 1992 am based at the Victoria Out- patient Clinic of Forensic Psychiatric Services, and provide consultations to the Vancouver Island Regional Correctional Centre.

I have testified at all levels of trial Courts in B.C., the Yukon and North West Territories. I also provide Psychiatric Assessments for the National Parole Board.

To date I have assessed more than 3000 individuals charged or convicted for a criminal offense. I have testified in Court about 300 times, and have taken part in more than one dozen Dangerous Offender proceedings.

I have extensive experience in Forensic Psychiatry, especially issues around the assessment of violent offenders, sexual offenders, substance- abusing offenders and a full range of mentally disordered offenders. Specific issues often addressed include mental state at time of offense, fitness for trial, general case management and future risk to the community.

<u>General Psychiatric Experience</u>:

Director of in-patient Psychiatric Unit at Yarmouth Regional Hospital(Nova Scotia) 1984-1985.Currently, small general private practice.

<u>Qualifications:</u>

Basic Medical training (MB, BS) in India, 1978. Subsequent qualifying examinations in Canada(MCCEE,1984;)

Residency in Psychiatry at UBC(1980-1984). Chief Resident, 1983. Six months of specific training in Forensic Psychiatry, 1984. Passed Fellowship exams (FRCP) at end of Residency and have been a Fellow of the Royal College of Physicians and Surgeons of Canada since 1984. Fully qualified to practice Medicine in B.C.

S. Lohrasbe, MB. BS, FRCP(C)

Briefly those were the credentials of our first expert witness and even more briefly his opinion;
At the time of the shooting Mr. Demers was in a " **dissociative state"**!
Normal mental functioning requires the coordination of several mental processes simultaneously so that the individual perceives his reality accurately, makes meaningful connections, generates appropriate choices and acts on them on the basis of his needs and desires. When there is a gross disruption in the integration of these processes- a dissociation- the individual is not functioning as a coherent, rational individual. Instead, one or more mental processes,

functioning independently, generate actions that are not in accord with the individual's overall desires, plans or intentions. Such a conceptualization is necessarily theoretical(it cannot be concretely demonstrated) but has a long and well-accepted genealogy within psychiatry! **Note: It's a lot like Evolution! (No one can prove it, but they know it's true) my opinion:**

Second Witness for the Defense: Robert G. Ley, Ph.D* Clinical and Consulting Psychologist.

Qualifications in Forensic Psychology
Since 1982, I have been registered to practice(clinical) psychology in B.C. (Reg.No. 855). I hold a Masters and Doctoral degrees in clinical psychology from the University of Waterloo, in Waterloo, Ontario. I was a Fellow in Psychology at the Langley Porter Psychiatric Institute at the University of California Medical School in San Francisco. Previously, I have held academic and clinical appointments in psychology at the Baylor College of Medicine and Texas Children's Hospital at the Texas Medical Centre in Houston Texas, where I also had a private practice.

At present, I am a tenured professor (rank: Associate Professor) in the psychology department at Simon Fraser University (SFU). At SFU, I teach graduate and undergraduate courses in psychological assessment, psychotherapy, personality theory, child and adolescent psychology, as well as ethics and professional issues. Also, I am the Director of Training of the Psychology and Law Institute of SFU.

Over the last ten years, I have consulted to a variety of forensic and correctional settings, including; the Lower Mainland Regional Correctional Center(LMRCC), the Willingdon Youth Detention Centre (YDC), the Burnaby, Community Correctional Centre (BCCC), the Youth Services to the Courts Clinic (YSC) of the Forensic Psychiatric

Services Commission, and the Regional Psychiatric Centre of the Correctional Services of Canada. In these consulting capacities, I have treated and assessed numerous criminal offenders, particularly sexual offenders, as well as other violent (non- sexual) adult and adolescent offenders.

Currently, I am a consultant to the RCMP, the Vancouver City Police, the National Parole Board, and the Crown Counsel Victim Services of the Region.

I have been often qualified as an expert witness for the defense and Crown Counsel in forensic, clinical, and child clinical psychology in the Provincial and Supreme Courts of B.C. Alberta, and Newfoundland. I have been designated an expert in Dangerous Offender proceedings. Since 1982, I have had a private practice in Vancouver, that is oriented towards forensic work and psychotherapy of adults, adolescents, and children.

Opinion: At the time Mr. Demers shot Mr. Lee, I believe that Mr. Demers was in an altered state of consciousness. I believe he was in a state of psychological disassociation, comparable to that which is often seen in battered spouses. In my view, Mr. Demers was depressed, fearful, and helpless at the time.

Both expert witnesses for the defense had independently reached the conclusion : **That at the time of the shooting , I was in a dissociative state!**

Interestingly the opinion expressed by these two learned doctors was exactly **opposite** to the opinion expressed by the expert witness for the Crown, Dr. Semrau.!?!

There it was...... two very nice neat professional opinions presented to the Court..... exactly opposite to the single presentation of the Crown's expert witness!

Tomorrow both the Crown and Defense would make their summations and closing arguments ..... Resting their cases! My throat was dry yet I was sweating bullets! As guilty as I felt at that moment, words cannot express how innocent I wanted to be! I wanted to be Not Guilty!........I had to be Not Guilty!!

July,18th,1996 (Day9) Both lawyers made their final summations to the Court. Mr. Schlosser, summarized all the evidence presented by the Crown, and reiterated why I should be found guilty!

Mr. Jackson, summarized all the evidence presented by both sides noting that the Crown had failed to prove intent.! He further noted that while provocation was no defense.... The repeated threats, harassment, lewd language and perverse conduct of Mr. Lee had over a sustained period of time caused a condition well known to the scientific community as, a " dissociative state" in my mind, making me incapable of consciously wanting to hurt Lee!

The jury was presented with a psychiatric explanation and would have to make their decision as to whether it was accurate or not!

The court was adjourned until the next day and everyone vacated the courtroom. Tomorrow was to be my day of judgment.... Would I be weighed in the scales and found wanting? I don't think I slept one wink that evening, as every imaginable thought possible flashed through my mind!

July 19th, 1996 (Day 10) As the Court reconvened the Honourable Judge Hamilton addressed the Court and Charged the Jury after which an adjournment was called as the Jury retired to decide the case. As we left the courthouse I was a nervous wreck, wanting to run somewhere but knowing there was no place to run!

Along with my family and some close friends we drove to the suite I was renting from John, my realtor friend, for coffee, where we would wait for the Jury as they decided my fate! We weren't there for longer than an hour when the telephone rang and we were informed the Jury had reached a verdict! We were instructed to return to the courthouse immediately!

I was incredulous, that this group of people could have reached a conclusion so quickly! As we drove back to the courthouse my heart was pounding so hard I thought my chest was going to burst! I was looking for somewhere to run, somewhere to hide, fighting back tears, trying to appear calm though I felt anything but!

Brian met us just in front of the courtroom and ushered me into the docket where I sat awaiting the judge and jury! This period of time just before the reconvening of the Court was the most difficult I have ever had to face! I can only imagine what eternal judgment will be like... I can only say you're all alone!

" All rise", Came the command, as the Judge entered the courtroom and seated himself at the bench.

" Has the Jury reached it's verdict"? he asked, to which the foreman of the jury stood and responded, " We have, your Honour".

The verdict: To the charge of attempted murder- **Not Guilty!**

To the charge of discharging a firearm with intent to injure- **Not Guilty!**

To the charge of using a firearm during the commission of an indictable offence- undetermined.

This was the unanimous decision of the Jury!

Ten to Fifteen seconds passed as everyone sat in stunned silence! Steven Lee leapt to his feet and stormed out of the courtroom followed by his wife. The Judge stood and left as the courtroom exploded with jubilation! The sheriff ushered me from the prisoner's docket where Brian met me and we embraced each other! I burst into tears of relief as I could feel Brian shaking beneath his flowing black robes! People lined up to shake my hand, among them a deputy and several jury members! Pats on the back and shouts of congratulations rained upon me from all around the courtroom!

Carol was in a sort of shock almost denial as her mind tried to interpret whether I was really innocent or was there some mistake? Gradually with Dianne's assurances Carol came to believe that indeed I had been found not guilty and was free to go. The whole affair seemed to come to an end so quickly and I couldn't help but marvel at how quickly the judge left the courtroom!

His job over, he was out of there! (and I mean **Now!**) One of the jurists waited a good twenty minutes to tell me that he had spoken passionately to his fellow members on my innocence, to my extreme gratification! It was gratifying to hear his opinion and how he believed in me! I guess I really needed to hear that someone felt what he was telling me.

We finally went for a victory lunch with our family, friends and our lawyers. This was a total victory for the defense team which would have many resounding implications in the legal field across Canada. Of course this victory wouldn't be bad for Brian's business either! I was later told that this case was studied in every university law class in our country!

Note: A similar case in Calgary involving a Mrs. Jodrey (charged with shooting her husband) resulted in her being placed under the care of psychiatrists in an institution. A year later in a telephone conversation with Brian Jackson, I was informed that the defense he had used was no longer available, in Canada.

Reflecting on the decision I have many times thought that **the jury wanted to set me free....** and my lawyer simply provided them with a way to do just that! I have been told how lucky I was..... And rightly so. Not a day goes by that I don't thank God for the decision that jury made!

My family and I were very grateful for the unanimous not guilty verdict of the jury as the reader might well imagine! Sure we had a our lives to put back together, bills to pay, and there was still the ongoing civil suit to deal with, but beyond that, I would keep my job and I wasn't going to jail!

Shortly after the trial, I hooked up our tent trailer to the truck, loaded up the kids and we left on a vacation to Washington, just to catch our breath and wallow in the freedom we had thought might be lost! What a wonderful time we had as we visited Portland and some of Oregon's beautiful coast ! Then it was up to Seattle and over to Whidbey Island where we just lazed around touring the state parks and the little towns at our own leisurely pace.

We returned through Bellingham and then up the scenic Chukanut Drive to British Columbia. As we headed home via the Coquihalla Highway we relished the reprieve our little excursion had provided. Now it was back to work as summer would quickly turn to fall.

We weren't home long when Brian called from his office in Vancouver to inform us that there had been no appeal launched by the Crown so the verdict would remain unchallenged and unchanged! In addition Brian informed us that I would have absolutely no record! We all agreed that he had done an admirable job as our lawyer!

Unfortunately things didn't go well between ourselves and Mr. Clarke, (Brian's friend) our civil lawyer. For some reason we were never able to communicate or bond with Mr. Clarke. Eventually it was mutually agreed that Ritchie Clarke would no longer act on our behalf, and we were left to our own resources.

Pretty much out of funds to pay a lawyer to defend us in the civil matters, I decided along with the help of a friend to handle my own legal case. A petition to the Court to force the Insurance company(which had insured our home) to defend me eventually failed after six years. This was a tremendous blow to us after spending so much time working on our presentation to the Court!

When the Court decided there was in fact no legal responsibility for the insurance company to pay for my legal expenses, it was only on a legal technicality! The decision was based on the fact that I had not filed the papers on time!!! What was so difficult to understand was that in fact the law firm representing the insurance company had stalled me while they pretended to negotiate with me.... All the time knowing full well that I had only one year to launch an action against their client!!

It didn't seem to matter that I had written to this law firm well within the time limit and asked if I should launch an action? I believed as legal representatives of the court, that law firm had a duty to disclose the truth to me particularly when I had asked them in writing! I believed this then and I still believe it today..... But there's no use kicking a dead dog!

The honorable judge rendered her decision and while it was open to appeal, I hadn't the money or constitution to continue! As soon as the decision was made by the Court, the Insurance company came after me for costs, which they had every reason to expect they were entitled to. I complained to the judge however that this decision was in error based on the law firm's refusal to disclose the truth when I asked in writing!

I think the judge felt a measure of sympathy for me as she found a reason to have each side pay their own legal costs! She wasn't satisfied the Insurance company representative had performed adequately. **Clearly God had his hand in this decision!** I had lost the case in court and by all rights legal costs should have fallen on me.....

Had I the money to launch an appeal, I would have done so, but by now I was beginning to see that there are no sure things in a court of law! I figured I would cut my losses and run!

There was still Steven Lee and his law suit to deal with, but amazingly my spirits were high as I prepared a case to present from the three foot high pile of legal papers I had accumulated over the years!

When his lawyer sent me any documents I would study them and try to find out what my options were from whatever sources were available. Sometimes I co-operated and sometimes I didn't, but as time passed I gradually built quite a good defense which I planned to present myself. I was always aware of the saying ,Whoever defends himself in court has an idiot for a client, but what choice did I have as I was virtually broke?

Sure I was paying my bills, but I couldn't afford a lawyer as my legal bills had topped **one hundred and fifty thousand dollars**! I had made the decision that you couldn't squeeze blood out of a stone and if I lost this case there wasn't going to be any money there for Lee anyway!

Eventually I was required to disclose all the documents I had to Lee's lawyer so that they would see how well prepared I was to go to court. This I did and then I waited for the first day of court to roll around. Shortly before the appointed court date, I received papers from Lee's lawyer asking what I was prepared to settle for?

My response was that if the plaintiff would drop his suit then I would drop our countersuit. I was elated when after several weeks they accepted my offer and the whole matter finally came to an abrupt end! I suppose Lee came to the conclusion that as there would be no insurance money for him and he could possibly lose the case in court, he would rather not risk spending any more money and open himself up to our countersuits if he lost!

The whole mess was finally over! After ten long years our legal ordeal had finally come to an end!!! **Praise The Lord!**

The Last Ten Years

—∽—

Much has happened between the criminal trial and the culmination of the civil suit. Over ten years have elapsed in each member of this family's life! To cover it all would be to lose sight of the real purpose of this book and turn it into a novel of epic proportions. I will try to bring the reader up to date by skimming some of the more salient and meaningful happenings in our lives.

In October of 1999, I had a severe heart attack, after a rather quick walk up Dilworth Mountain! Dianne, telephoned for an ambulance and as she was a registered nurse managed to have no less than two teams of paramedics show up simultaneously! The doctors commented that had I been five minutes longer getting to the hospital, I would have been taken to the morgue instead! **I guess it wasn't my time?! Thank - you Dianne! Maybe I'll finish this book yet?**

In July of 2001, I was feeling poorly and after running the appropriate tests it was determined that I was in need of a coronary bypass operation! After a two week stay in our Kelowna hospital waiting for an operation to be scheduled I was finally offered my choice of either flying to Seattle immediately or to Vancouver two days later. I chose to stay in Canada and have the operation at Vancouver General. I am Canadian, and simply felt more comfortable having the procedure done here. Judging by the results I think I made the right decision!

I had a successful triple heart bypass operation with absolutely no complications whatsoever! The staff at Vancouver General were first class all the way. While recuperating there over the next 5 days I came upon a chess playing acquaintance of mine quite by accident, who was in the hospital in a dreadful state! Gerry had been stricken by a very strange virus while he was at the Abbotsford airport waiting to fly out to a chess tournament.

The virus struck him both motionless and speechless leaving him in this state for the best part of one year! That's absolutely true as difficult as the reader might find it to believe! Gerry was in Vancouver General Hospital for one full year while the medical staff tended to his every need nursing him back to health!

The day I happened to see him there he couldn't move or speak as four nurses were tending to his every need! Seeing him in that state I must state that I never thought he would survive this terrible ordeal! To the credit of the medical staff Gerry completely recovered with few side effects and was able to return to his championship chess play! When I saw him several years later, at a chess tournament, I asked him if at any time he had felt like giving up and simply dying? He began to cry and very movingly told me that yes he had prayed for death! I must say I don't for a moment blame him as I thought him worse than dead at the time I saw him! **Life is strange, isn't it?**

In November of 2002, we received a phone call that my wife's sister Elizabeth and her husband David Bush had been horribly and brutally murdered in their Kamloops home! As this terrible story unfolded over the next few days their only son Christopher was also found shot to death in his parents car on a forest road outside town! It was later established that Christopher had in fact committed suicide after murdering his parents!What a tragic end for the Bush family who were survived by two daughters Jennifer and Alexis!(not at home at the time).While there is no way to adequately explain a tragedy such as this, time has a way of mitigating it's effect. Both Jennifer and Alexis,(our nieces), while not forgetting their past have moved on with their lives. They are both married, and mothers of their own children, living productive lives. The reader may recall that my criminal lawyer, Mr. Brian Jackson and my now deceased brother in law David Bush, had grown up next door to one another in Trail, B.C. going through school together. David had called Brian and asked him to contact Carol and offer to defend me! **Life is so strange, isn't it?**

In October, of 2003, Carol's father, Tom Fusick, passed away, after an unsuccessful battle against cancer! He was a self educated finishing carpenter and cabinet maker, a designer, and a very giving man! It was very hard for Carol to lose her father so soon after the tragic loss of her sister, Elizabeth!

Harder still for Carol was the loss of her younger brother Tommy not six months later in March of 2004 to cancer! Life is not fair, nor is it easy to comprehend ?! There was no way for me to understand how such a wonderful woman as my wife should have to face loss after loss!

Tommy's untimely death was followed by the death of yet another sister, Susan in October, of 2004!Susan had chronic leukemia most of her adult life and many other complications which stemmed from this blood disorder, but it's never easy to lose a loved sister!Susan was survived by her husband Daryll and daughter Dianne Shannon both of Dallas, Texas! While Tommy was survived by his wife Betty and their surviving children Ryan, Dawn and Kim living in the lower mainland of British Columbia, Canada. These tragedies following in rapid succession were extremely difficult for Carol , but to her credit, she accepted it as best a person could under the circumstances and continues trying to live a victorious Christian life! Carol's immediate surviving family members David, (who has already lost a leg to cancer) Darlene (her youngest sister)and Carol's mother(Edith) are all that remain of her family from the time I began dating her! Fortunately the three all live in Kelowna and can get together whenever they wish. Again I say...... **Isn't life strange?**

During my convalescence from the heart operation, Telus, (formally B. C. Telephone Co.) offered a retirement package to employees age 55+. With no hesitation whatsoever I jumped at the offer and retired from the company I had joined in 1965! What a wonderful career I had over thirty six years working and traveling all over supernatural British Columbia! I met so many interesting characters and had so many laughs, that it would take a second book to recount all the splendid stories locked in my memory!

Each of our children (all eight) have grown, and one by one have left our little nest! In the beginning while it was difficult for Carol and I to adjust to, we resigned ourselves to this commonly accepted fact of life! In the normal scheme of things, our children grow, and begin making small forays out into the world..... Until they are actually fully and totally ...... gone! We always knew we were training them up to leave, but now they are all gone! Our home is empty, and I feel so alone as I type these lines! It is the most difficult part of life that we have had to endure so far! We loved those kids so much, so very, very much, but they're gone. They were our glue..... Our reason for staying together..... They gave us purpose, a reason to get up each day, and to come home every night!

Of course we still see them, get together for meals and picnics, or little shopping trips, or perhaps working on things around their homes, but it isn't the same really. They aren't ours anymore; they are their own. They have mates, husbands, wives, boyfriends, girlfriends, and many times not partners we would necessarily have chosen for them. Sometimes things don't work out, and the next time we see them they might be with someone else. Then it's up to Carol and I to try to accept the changes and adapt. **Life is so strange!**

The house that always seemed so small, now seems much larger than it really has to be. We're always throwing out food that spoils because we only learned how to purchase in bulk, because of the size of our family. Slowly Carol and I are learning how to cope with this quiet home lifestyle which I suppose is much the same as it was when the two of us started out!

After about three years of retirement, playing chess and writing at the computer, I have taken a job with the Commissionaires. It's a large security organization comprised of retired servicemen and policemen as well as people who still want something to do. It fills some of my spare time with purpose. I guess if a person isn't sick or dying, they should stay busy living! Carol is still working at London Drugs, and both she and I will file for our Canada Pension soon!

Through all the trials of this life our God has sustained us, for which we thank him! We feel fortunate indeed to have been given the gift of life and to have enjoyed being able to live it in Canada! We have been blessed beyond measure and look forward to the second Advent of our Lord!

ROY J. DEMERS - SPITFIRE MK VIII   "S"

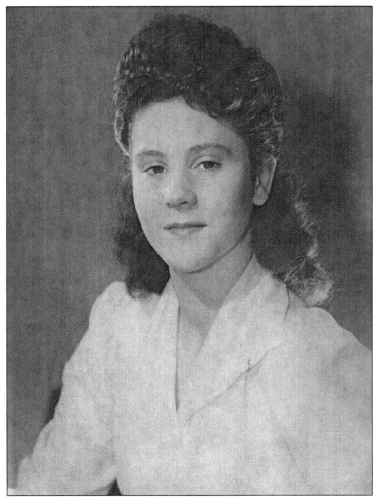

Doreen (Martin) Demers

Warne Soyland and I Return from Arizona

Top - "The Starfires- Prince George- 65
Bottom Left- "Riverside Review"-
accompanying-Carol Fusick
Bottom Right- "Starfires" CKBI TV Prince Albert

Prime Minister of Canada- Rt. Honorable John Diefenbaker and wife Olive Diefenbaker.

Demers- Fusick wedding- Sept. 07, 68.- Terrace, B.C.

Diving and other activities around Lasquiti Island,
while on our sailing trip in the Gulf Islands.

B)- Visiting with the Johnson's aboard
their beautiful sailboat.

C) The "Campella" our rental boat, after running aground on Iona Sewage Banks our final day of sailing.

B)- Visiting with the Johnsons aboard
their beautiful sailboat.

Starline Farms- Saskatoon

Demers Children- 95

Carol- Dianne- Darwin

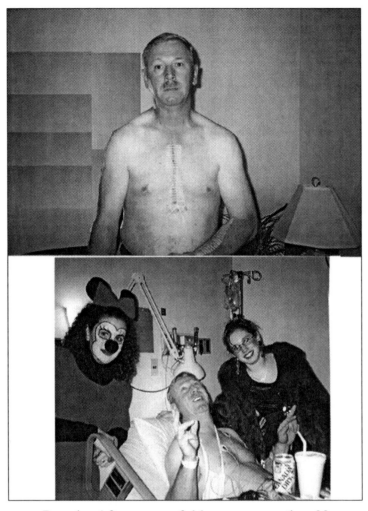

Darwin- After successful by-pass operation-02
Get well visit- Lori and Lesley-
after my heart attack- Oct. 99

'Silly' feud sparks shooting
Neighbors say children at root of dispute

GARY MOORE/*The Daily Courier*
Three Mounties handcuff a man accused of shooting his neighbor with a shotgun in Glenrosa Monday afternoon. Police used tracking dogs and a helicopter to find the 47-year-old man. Darwin David De-

By DON PLANT and J.P. SQUIRE
The Daily Courier

A neighborhood dispute left a Glenrosa man fighting for his life after he was shot three times with a shotgun Monday afternoon.

A 47-year-old man faces charges of attempted murder after Steven Lee, 35, was shot in the chest, the upper thigh and hand about 4 p.m. Lee was seriously injured but is expected to survive.

Neighbors say Lee and a friend had been cutting firewood in the bush above Woodell Road in Glenrosa for a couple days before the attack. The pair was walking back along a gravel road toward Woodell Road when they were confronted by a neighbor carrying a 12-gauge shotgun.

Lee and the neighbor exchanged words, and Lee was shot.

The suspect ran into the bush above Woodell Road and police called in tracking dogs and a helicopter to flush him out.

Officers arrested him and recovered a shotgun about an hour later.

A wheelbarrow containing

GARY NYLANDER/*The Daily Courier*
An RCMP officer guards the scene with a shotgun on Woodell Road after a man charged with shooting his neighbor fled to a nearby wooded area. He was later caught.

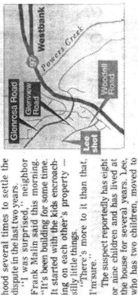

mers faces several charges, including attempted murder, and was expected to appear in court today.

chopped wood was lying on its side on the gravel road near the suspect's house this morning.

The shooting was the climax of a long, ongoing dispute between the next-door neighbors over "problems with children and youth problems," said RCMP Staff Sgt. Darryl Graves. Officers have been called to the Glenrosa neighborhood several times to settle the dispute in the last two years.

"I was surprised," neighbor Frank Malin said this morning. "It's been building for some time. It started with the kids encroaching on each other's property — silly little things.

"There's more to it than that, I'm sure."

The suspect reportedly has eight or nine children and has lived at the house for several years. Lee, who has two children, moved to the neighborhood in 1991.

"It's a friendly enough neighborhood, but residents don't interfere with each other," said Margaret Malin. "To shoot someone is going a little too far."

Senior investigators drove to Kelowna General Hospital hoping to interview Lee this morning.

The suspect, Darwin David Demers, faces charges of attempted murder, discharging a firearm with intent, and other gun-related offences. He was held overnight and was expected to appear in court today.

WEDNESDAY, JANUARY 4, 1995

FREE WITH THE DAILY COURIER

Neighbors' feud leads to shooting

Police call on helicopter to help capture a suspect after three shots are fired in fight between residents in Glenrosa

WESTSIDE RCMP helped outfit the dogman before conducting a search in the Glenrosa area. A 47-year-old suspect has been arrested and charged following a shooting in the community.

Man out on bond in shooting case

OKAN
THE OKANAGAN SUN

KELOWNA — Friends and relatives hugged and shook hands moments after a Westbank man charged with attempted murder was ordered released from custody on Friday.

Their elation contrasted with the demeanor of Darwin David Demers, who wept quietly in the prisoner's dock throughout the hour-long bail hearing in provincial court as 20 of his family members looked on.

The 48-year-old B.C. Tel employee was let out of jail on a $50,000 bond three hours after Judge Bill Selbie ordered his release. Demers' son-in-law posted the bond minutes after the hearing.

Conditions of Demers' release included him staying away from Steven Lee, the 32-year-old neighbor he's charged with shooting three times with a shotgun on Monday afternoon.

Lee was taken to Kelowna General Hospital with gunshot wounds to his shoulder, hand and leg, and was listed in critical condition on Monday. He's been upgraded to stable condition, but remains an intensive care.

Demers must also have no contact with Lee's wife and two children, and stay out of Westbank un-

less he travels along Highway 97 through town.

Defence lawyer Brian Jackson spent 30 minutes arguing for Demers' release and submitted nearly 80 letters attesting to his client's character. A ban on publication forbids details of the hearing to be printed.

Neighbors say Lee and a friend had been cutting firewood in the bush above Woodell Road in Westbank and were walking near Demers' house Monday afternoon when a man shot Lee with a 12-gauge shotgun at close range.

The woman ran into the bush and police called in tracking dogs and a helicopter to find him. Demers was arrested about 90 minutes later.

People who know Demers and Lee told reporters they'd been feuding since Lee moved to Woodell Road in 1992. Police were called several times and had to break up a street fight between the men last fall.

Described as a "non-smoking, non-drinking Christian" and devoted family man, Demers is also president of the Kelowna chess club. He and his wife have eight children.

He is scheduled to appear in court again on Jan. 26.

Darwin David Demers and his daughter Janice walk away from the court building on Water Street in Kelowna minutes after he was released from custody on a $50,000 bond Friday afternoon. Demers is charged with attempted murder after he was alleged to have shot his Westbank neighbor Steven Lee three times with a shotgun Monday.

48 CAPITAL NEWS, Wednesday, January 4, 1995

Neighborhood feud erupts into shooting

By Darshan Lindsay
STAFF WRITER

A 47-year-old Glenrosa man was expected to appear in court late Tuesday afternoon on charges in connection with a shooting in Glenrosa Monday.

Police received a call shortly after 4 p.m. of a man being shot on Woodell Road.

On arrival, they found that a 35-year-old man had been shot three times by his neighbor. The man was rushed to hospital with serious injuries, but they were not considered life-threatening.

Police searched the wooded area surrounding Woodell Road with police dogs and a helicopter and found the suspect in some bush at approximately 5:30 p.m. They also found a shotgun.

Police say the incident was a result of a long-standing dispute between the neighbors which has required police intervention before.

"It's something that's been on-going. We've been involved in the past," said RCMP Insp. Dick Smith.

47-year-old Darwin Demers is charged in connection with the shooting. He faces several charges, including attempted murder.

KELOWNA & AREA
THE DAILY COURIER

WEDNESDAY, JULY 12, 1995

Shotgun victim recovers slowly

A carpenter by trade, Steve Lee has been forced to sell down his tools while he recovers from injuries suffered in a Jan. 2 shooting outside his home.

Steven Lee is thankful his injuries suffered in a Jan. 2 shooting weren't worse

BY DON PLANT
The Daily Courier

WESTBANK — Three operations and six months of rehabilitation later, Steven Lee is still recovering from three gunshot blasts that nearly killed him.

Lee, 35, was hit with a 12-gauge shotgun at close range outside his Glenrosa home Jan. 2 as he and a friend collected firewood. He was hit in the upper chest, hand and thigh, but managed to stagger into his home without collapsing.

After weeks in hospital and countless hours of therapy, Lee still can't make a fist with his left hand, has trouble raising his arms, and feels pain throughout his body. The worst damage may be psychological.

"When I hear something outside, I don't go to the window," he said Monday. "I go out the back door

and walk around. I don't sleep at night."

Each shotgun shell contains 350 steel pellets. Most of the 1,000-plus beatings are still inside Lee and will likely remain there the rest of his life.

Luckily, not one of the pellets hit his heart or spine. One of the shots narrowly missed a major artery.

"The specialists were totally amazed," Lee said. "The pellets grazed all the soft tissue out of the way and formed protective barriers around the main artery. If one pellet hit it, I would have been dead in 10 minutes."

Lee was pushing a wheelbarrow near his house on Woodell Road when a man holding a shotgun came out from behind a hedge. He said the man threatened to kill him, aimed the gun at his head and pulled the trigger.

"The safety was on, so the man released it and fired again, striking Lee in the upper right chest, he said.

"I dropped the wheelbarrow and ran down the hill ... with my back to him, I got another shot - he

wiped out my hand, my elbow and part of my fanny (when driver).

"I was running for my life," Lee said. "I kept running with my whole shoulder stumped. My daughter ran out, so I said 'Get in, get in!' I turned around to see where he was. He was standing there, pointing. He let it go and hit me in the leg.

Lee assembled his family while his friend called 911. He doesn't remember much after the ambulance took him to Kelowna General Hospital.

In the weeks that followed, doctors operated twice on Lee's chest and once on his hand. Lee still has six to eight more weeks of rehabilitation to complete, but it could take 18 months before he makes a full recovery. Still, he's grateful his condition isn't worse.

"It was just lucky I didn't die or become paralyzed," he said.

Darwin David Demers, 48, was charged with attempted murder and gun-related offences. He was released on $50,000 bail and is scheduled for a three-day preliminary hearing in September.

197

Shooting victim denies provoking attack

By Darshan Lindsay
STAFF WRITER

The victim of a serious shooting in Glenrosa last year denies having provoked his attacker.

Taking the stand at the attempted murder trial of Darwin David Demers, Steven Lee said he was not responsible for the tension between himself and his former Woodell Road neighbor.

"I did nothing wrong, sir, to be shot," said Lee, responding to a barrage of questions from Demers' lawyer, Brian Jackson, on Wednesday.

"Did you tell anyone in the hospital (after the shooting) 'I just pushed him too far'?" asked Jackson.

"No. Definitely not, sir," replied Lee.

Jackson asked, "Have you ever threatened any member of the Demers family?"

"No sir, never sir."

"Have you ever directed any foul language at any member of the Demers family?"

"No."

Lee's testimony was in stark contrast to what the court heard the day before from members of the Demers family and a boarder who said they felt like prisoners in their home.

In their testimony Lee was painted as a bully who wouldn't stop harassing the family.

Demers has pleaded not guilty to a charge of attempted murder arising from an incident on Jan. 2, 1995. The 48-year-old is accused of shooting Lee three times, sending him to hospital with injuries to his chest, left arm and hand, and left thigh. Lee testified he thought Demers was joking around when the man approached him outside his residence, armed with a shotgun.

"The first thing he said to me was, 'I'm going to kill you, I've had enough.' … I thought the man was fooling."

When the first round of shot struck his chest, Lee said he thought he was going to die.

During his testimony, Lee admitted he had problems with his neighbors which he claims began with a smashed pumpkin on Hallowe'en night in 1993.

Believing one of the Demers children was responsible, Lee asked Darwin to deal with it.

To his knowledge, nothing was ever done, and Lee got increasingly frustrated.

RCMP were called to the Woodell Road neighborhood on two occasions in 1994 as a result of two disputes between the families. One of them involved a fist fight between the two men.

The trial in B.C. Supreme Court in Kelowna is expected to continue into next week.

Kelowna CITIZEN

CAPITAL NEWS, Wednesday, July 17, 1996 A3

Neighbor tormented accused, wife says

By Darshan Lindsay
STAFF WRITER

The wife of a man charged with trying to kill his former neighbor recounted years of torment at the hands of the victim.

Testifying Monday at the attempted murder trial of her husband, Darwin David Demers, Carol Demers described incident after incident of a neighbor who continually harassed her family.

"You could never get away from him. He was always there," said Carol of Steven Lee.

Her husband is accused of shooting the man three times on Jan. 2, 1995, sending him to hospital with serious, but not life-threatening, injuries.

After arresting Demers, RCMP said the incident was the result of a simmering neighborhood dispute. According to Carol, trouble between the families began soon after the Lees moved in next door to their Woodell Road home in the spring of 1992.

An angry Steven Lee would frequently pound on the Demers' front door over reported problems between the families' children.

"Mr. Lee, with every instance, would step in accusing that it was always my children doing something. He demeaned me all the time as a mom," said Carol recalling her neighbor even called her a "slut on one occasion.

"Once he told me I had too many kids, that I must be a … that went," said Carol.

The Demers' have eight children.

The jury hearing the case in B.C. Supreme Court in Kelowna was told the name-calling and harassment from Lee reached the point where the Demers family would avoid any contact with their neighbor; the children were told to walk on the other side of the street and the Demers kept the curtains on the windows facing Lee's home closed most of the time.

"The threats (from Lee) became death threats over time and he always told us he hated us and we never knew why … He said we'd better sleep with one eye open and never turn our back," said Carol through tears.

She said in 1994 Darwin refused to take the family away on holiday, fearing the safety of his own home, and the couple began to take a serious look at moving. Carol said it was the only thing that would bring peace.

During cross-examination, Crown prosecutor Jerold Schlosser said he found it peculiar the Demers family never once made a formal complaint about the death threats allegedly made by Steven Lee.

Carol Demers finished her testimony Monday afternoon and was one of several witnesses scheduled to be called by the defence this week. Darwin Demers is also expected to take the stand.

JULY 20, 1996

KELOWNA COURTS

Shooting victim wounded again

■ Neighbor acquitted of attempted murder

By JOHN KEERY
The Okanagan Saturday

KELOWNA — Steven Lee says he was on trial in B.C. Supreme Court for the past two weeks, not the man who shot him three times with a shotgun.

A jury yesterday found Darwin David Demers, 49, not guilty of attempted murder and the lesser offences of assault with intent to wound, and assault causing bodily harm.

Lee, 36, said the defence painted him as the villain, not Demers, his former neighbor in Glenrosa who shot him Jan. 2, 1996.

"It seems the system told them I deserved it," Lee said. "What would have happened if he would have killed me."

Demers could not be reached for comment af-

ter the shooting so the two families are no longer neighbors. The court was told of a long running state of animosity between the neighboring families.

The Demers family claimed Lee harassed Demer's wife Carol and some of his eight children, threatening to blow up their house and shoot them.

Lee said Demers' eldest son, David, threw rocks at his house and on lawns he was mowing for his landscaping business.

He said he never had any dealings with Demers himself except for a fist fight in 1994 and the shooting incident.

The story the Demers family and friends told the court about him harassing them was untrue, Lee said.

"It seemed like they (the jury) had their minds made up a long time ago."

Lee said he still suffers from the shotgun wounds he received to his chest, arm and hand and will require at least one more operation.

"I still have pellets coming out of my armpit and my left hand," he said. "I have nerve damage to my hand and my fingers are shattered."

Even if he was as bad as defence lawyer Brian Jackson tried to portray him, Lee said, that should not give his neighbor licence to shoot him.

"It is very scary in our system when a man can use a shotgun, stalk his neighbor like an animal, then say he didn't remember," Lee said. "There is a loose cannon out there and somebody (else) is going to get it one day."

Demers told the court he was not in control of his actions at the time of the shooting. It was like two parts of him, a dominant and a passive part, doing verbal battle, he said.

Some psychiatrists accept this as a legitimate condition which sometimes affects people in severe trauma, such as rape victims.

Two psychiatrists who testified offered opposing opinions on the validity of the condition, known as a dissociative state.

Crown prosecutor Jerold Schlosser said he has 30 days to appeal.

He said he will wait until at least next week to decide if an appeal is reasonable.

Schlosser said the jury was very attentive and seemed to be well aware of the issues.

Judge Howard Hamilton told 12 the jurors they must not consider the character of either Demers or Lee in reaching their decision.

He stressed that they must find Demers not guilty if there was any reasonable doubt he actually decided to and attempted to kill or injure Lee.

199

THE COURTS

Neighbor didn't intend to kill

A Glenrosa man who shot his neighbor after a long-running feud, didn't intend to kill him, a jury decided last week.

The jury found Darwin Demers, 49, not guilty of attempted murder and also acquitted him on lesser charges of assault with intent to wound, maim or, disfigure and assault causing bodily harm.

Demers took out a shotgun Jan. 2, 1996, and fired three shots at his Glenrosa neighbor, Steven Lee, causing a chest wound doctors say could have been fatal.

Although the reasons for the verdict in the B.C. Supreme Court trial in Kelowna were not given, it appears the jury accepted the argument that Demers wasn't in control of his actions.

The jury heard that Demers' family had been threatened many times by their neighbor.

After the trial, Lee said it appeared as if he was on trial not Demers.

"It seems the system told them I deserved it," Lee said. "What would have happened if he would have killed me?"

The story the Demers family and friends told the court about Lee harassing them was untrue, Lee said.

Lee said he still suffers from the shotgun wounds he received to his chest, arm and hand and will require at least one more operation.

"I still have pellets coming out of my armpit and my left hand," he said. "I have nerve damage to my hand and my fingers are shattered."

"It's very scary, our system, when a man can use a shotgun, stalk his neighbor like an animal, then say he didn't remember," Lee said. "There is a loose cannon out there and somebody (else) is going to get it one day."

Demers told the court he was not in control of his actions at the time of the shooting. Some psychiatrists accept this as a legitimate condition that can affect people in severe trauma.

Victoria forensic psychiatrist Shahedran Lahrasbe testified Demers was in a dissociative

Westside Weekly

Steven Lee, left, and Darwin Demers leave the Kelowna Law Courts building after a day of testimony last week.

state when he went to a closet, took out a shotgun, then went outside and shot at Lee.

"A person in a dissociative state is not capable of intending his actions. Various parts of the mental function are disconnected from one another."

Also, Demers did not appear to be in a rage, Lahrasbe said.

Demers testified that after he shot Lee, he sat in the bush with the shotgun and contemplated shooting himself.

Lahrasbe said Demers told him that a mental battle was going on in his head between his passive and aggressive self. The aggressive self won and he took the shotgun.

Lahrasbe said this is typical of people in a

dissociative state.

If Demers had simply lost his temper, he would have still have been angry after the incident, Lahrasbe said. He would not likely have tried to kill himself.

In his charge to the jury, Justice Howard Hamilton seemed to accept the disassociative state argument as a legitimate defence.

Hamilton told the jury it must find Demers not guilty unless it can reach a unanimous decision that he intended to kill Lee.

"The Crown must prove Demers intended to kill Lee and shot the shotgun in an attempt to do so," Hamilton said.

A psychiatrist for the prosecution tried to argue against the notion of a dissociative state as an established psychiatric phenomenon.

The incident occurred after more than a year and a half of problems between the neighbors. Lee, 36, is alleged to have repeatedly made threats to Demers, his wife Carol and their eight children.

Demers said he lost control but was not angry when he took out his shotgun, loaded it with bird shot, confronted Lee and fired three shots as Lee tried to run away.

"At that point my mind snapped," Demers said. "I felt I was an observer of what was happening the whole time. I was just recording sights and sounds."

Demers was watching a hockey game the day after New Year's, 1996, when his wife came and said Lee had made an obscene gesture to her. Demers said that set him off and he pulled out his shotgun.

He said he only intended to scare Lee, not kill him and was not aware Lee had been injured.

Crown prosecutor Jerold Schlosser said Demers should have called police whenever he was threatened, something he didn't do.

The Crown has 30 days to appeal the decision.

The Demers family moved to another location after the shooting so the two families are no longer neighbors.

JUSTICE | A4 CAPITAL NEWS, Sunday, July 21, 1996

Demers found not guilty

By Darshan Lindsay
Staff writer

Darwin David Demers walked from the Kelowna courthouse a freeman Friday.

He regained his freedom after a seven-man, five-woman jury took just an hour to reach its not guilty verdict, thus acquitting the former Glenrosa man on a charge of attempted murder.

For three weeks the 48-year-old father of eight children sat in B.C. Supreme Court listening to evidence mounted in the trial against him.

The Crown accused him of intentionally trying to kill his neighbor Steven Lee on Jan. 2,

1995. But Demers' lawyer, Brian Jackson, argued that Demers finally snapped after more than two years of harassment from the victim, and was not aware of, or in control of his actions due to a temporary moment of insanity.

On the afternoon of Jan. 2 Lee and a friend were wrapping up a day of hauling firewood from the woods near his Woodell Road neighborhood when Lee was approached by a gun-toting Demers.

According to evidence heard at the trial, Demers shot Lee three times with his shotgun, striking his chest, left arm and hand, and left thigh.

Lee spent several days in hospital recovering from the injuries.

In his own testimony, Lee flatly denied he did anything to provoke the attack.

However, witnesses called by the defence last week painted a much different picture of a neighbor who continually harassed the Demers family with insults and glaring looks. Family members recounted how they felt like prisoners in their own home.

One of the Demers children recalled how Lee had taken the joy of living from her parents. The young woman said she feared for their safety in light of death threats made by Lee.

In his final summation to the jury, Demers' lawyer told the jury it was Lee who drove the accused to the breaking point.

In his final address to the jury Thursday afternoon and Friday morning, B.C. Supreme Court Justice Howard Hamilton told the 12 men and women their role was not to determine who was good or bad neighbour, but whether Demers wanted to and intended to kill his neighbor.

In addition to acquitting Demers on the charge of attempted murder, the jury found him not guilty on a charge of using a firearm while committing an offence. The jury also found Demers not guilty on a charge of pointing a firearm, trying to wound, maim or disfigure Lee with his firearm.

CAPITAL NEWS, Friday, July 19, 1996 **A15**

Jury must decide if Demers in control of his own actions

By Darshan Lindsay
Staff writer

Lawyers in the Darwin David Demers attempted-murder trial agree the case is tragic.

However, prosecutor Jerald Schlosser said the remaining confrontations and stress between the accused and his former Woodell Road neighbour,

Steven Lee, did not give Demers the right to shoot.

In his final arguments in B.C. Supreme Court in Kelowna Thursday morning, Schlosser warned the seven-man, five-woman jury to keep each issue called by the defence throughout the week which suggested Demers snapped and wasn't aware

of what he was doing when he shot Lee three times on Jan. 2, 1995. Schlosser argued the 48-year-old father of eight children knew what he was doing.

Schlosser summed up his case after Brian Jackson, the lawyer for Demers, had his turn at the jury.

Jackson called the accused a man who

reached a breaking point and temporarily went insane. Jackson said it was a bully of a neighbor, who constantly harassed and threatened the family, that drove Demers to the breaking point. He said had Demers intended to kill Lee he would have used real slugs and not the number six bird shot

which left his 36-year-old neighbor with serious but non-life-threatening injuries.

According to Demers' own testimony earlier in the week, he said he went to the scene to talk to Lee about his harassment of his family.

A forensic psychiatrist called by the defence

Wednesday suggested Demers had been in a dissociative state at the time of the shooting, and as a result would not have been aware of or in control of his actions.

However, earlier in the trial a psychiatrist called by the Crown had a different view, believing Demers was aware of his actions.

Endnotes:

—✺—

Report: Stanley Semrau, - MD FRCPC Psychiatrist

Report: Robert G. Ley, PhD- Clinical and Consulting Psychologist

Report: Dr. S. Lohrasbe- MB, B S. FRCP) Forensic Psychiatrist

Report: D. Michael Bain, August,1996.

Report: News Media , Pictures, and Miscellaneous Materials.

January 12, 1995

Personnel Department
B.C. Telephone Company
Kelowna, B.C.

RE: Darwin Demers
D.O.B. 22-01-47

I have carried out a psychiatric assessment of Mr. Demers involving interviews with him on January 3, 1995. I have assessed him both with regard to his recent legal difficulties involving an attack on his neighbor and his general current mental health.

Except for an understandable and limited degree of stress associated with his legal difficulties, Mr. Demers is currently in good mental health. He suffers from mild anxiety symptoms but is not suffering from any significant depression not any other psychiatric complaints of any importance. He is not undergoing any specific psychiatric treatment and is not in need of any.

In my opinion he is not in any way a danger to his co-workers or to the public at large. The incident with his neighbor was highly out of character for him and was very specifically the result of particular difficulties between the two of them. Mr. Demers' behavior in that situation, while obviously alarming, does not reflect any general tendency or danger to be violent to other people.

Mr. Demers' current emotional state makes him fit to return to work. His thought and perceptual capacities are entirely intact and he exhibits good capabilities in attention, concentration, memory and judgment. It is possible that he may be subject to brief preoccupation from time to time due to his legal difficulties, but this would interfere with his work no more than any other employee who might be worried about their children or have just recently had a spat with their spouse.

Mr. Demers indicates a keen interest in returning to work as well as a feeling of responsibility to B.C. Tel and to his family to carry on with his employment commitments. I believe that work would also be healthy for him in channeling his energies and attention into concentration on his duties.

In summary, I have no reservations regard Mr. Demers' return to work and in my opinion he is entirely medically fit to do so. Please feel free to contact me if any further information is required.

Yours Sincerely,

Stanley Semrau, MD FRCPC
Psychiatrist

SS/cs

Robert G. Ley, Ph.D.
Clinical and Consulting Psychologist

Qualifications in Forensic Psychology

Since 1982, I have been registered to practice (clinical) psychology in B.C. (Registration No. 855). I hold Masters and Doctoral degrees in clinical psychology from the University of Waterloo, in Waterloo Ontario. I was a Fellow in Psychology at the Langley Porter Psychiatric Institute at the University of California Medical School in San Francisco. Previously, I have held academic and clinical appointments in psychology at the Baylor College of Medicine and Texas Children's Hospital at the Texas Medical Centre in Houston Texas, where I also had a private practice.

At present, I am a tenured professor (rank: Associate Professor) in the psychology department at Simon Fraser University (SFU). At SFU, I teach graduate and undergraduate courses in psychological assessment, psychotherapy, personality theory, child and adolescent psychology, as well as ethics and professional issues. Also, I am the Director of Training of the Psychology and Law Institute of SFU.

Over the last ten year, I have consulted to a variety of forensic and correctional settings, including; the Lower Mainland Regional Correctional Centre (LMRCC)m the Willingdon Youth Detention Centre (YDC), the Burnaby, Community Correctional Center (BCCC), the Youth Service to the Courts Clinic (YSC) of the Forensic Psychiatric Services Commission, and the Regional Psychiatric Centre of the Correctional Servies of Canada. In these consulting capacities, I have treated and assessed numerous criminal offenders, particularly sexual offends, as well as other violent (non-sexual) adult and adolescent offenders.

Currently, I am a consultant to the RCMP, the Vancouver City Police, the National Parole Board, and the Crown Counsel Victim Services of the Vancouver Region.

I have been often qualified as an expert witness for defense and Crown Counsel in forensic, clinical, and child clinical psychology in the Provincial and Supreme Courts of B.C., Alberta, and Newfoundland. I have bee designated and expert in Dangerous Offender proceedings. Since 1982, I have had a private practice in Vancouver, that is oriented towards forensic work and psychotherapy of adults, adolescents and children.

Robert G. Ley, Ph.D.
Clinical and Consulting Psychologist
April 10, 1996

Mr. J. Brian Jackson
Barrister and Solicitor
Suite 1502
Sun Tower- 100 W. Pender Street
Vancouver, BC
V6B 1R8

Dear Mr. Jackson:

RE: Regina v, Darwin DEMERS

At your request, I met with your client, 49 year old Mr.
Darwin Demers (date of birth: January 22, 1947) for the
purposes of conduction an assessment of his personality
and psychological functioning. Mr. Demers has been
charged with attempted murder, and he awaits trial on
this matter later this month. He has pleaded not guilty.
Mr. Demers is accused of shooting (with a shotgun) his
neighbor Mr. Steven Lee. In this assessment, you have
asked me to evaluate Mr. Demers' state of mind at the time
of this alleged offense. Additionally, you have asked me to
comment upon Mr. Demers' capacity to form intent, at the
time that he shot Mr. Lee.

Mr. Demers' current charge evolved from an incident on
January 2, 1995 in Mr. Demers' and Mr. Lee's neighborhood in Westbank. Their houses are adjacent, and there
has been much conflict between them over the last three
years, since Mr. Lee and his family moved next door to Mr.
Demers and his family. The shooting of Mr. Lee appears to
have been triggered by his making aggressive and obscene

gestures towards Mr. Demers' wife, Carol-Ann. According to Mr. Demers, he was watching (with his son, Mark) a television broadcast of the Canada vs. Russia world junior hockey championship. As he went towards the kitchen, he heard his wife exclaim to their tenant and friend (Ms. Diane Roth), that Mr. Lee was rudely gesturing towards her. Thereupon, Mr. Demers got his shotgun, and eventually he confronted and shot Mr. Lee. In the aftermath of the shooting Mr. Demers was suicidal. He walked in to the woods adjacent to the neighborhood, with the intention of shooting himself. He reports that he put the barrel of the shotgun into his mouth, but that he was unable to reach and discharge the trigger. Mr. Demers remained in the woods, until the police arrived, to take him into custody. Mr. Demers did not resist apprehension. Mr. Demers states that he was a very vague or "patchy' memory for many of the actions and events that attributed to him, in the context of the shooting of Mr. Lee. Mr. Demers does not believe that he was in conscious control ot his actions. He was not under the influence of alcohol or drugs at the time of the critical incident.

RE: DEMERS Darwin
Page 2

Background Information

At the time of this critical incident, as I have noted above, Mr. Demers, his wife Carol-Ann, and six of their eight children were residing in their Westbank home, where they had lived for about 15 years. Two of their young adult children had left home, and were living on their own. Darwin and Carol-Ann had been married for about 26 years at the time of this incident. Their friend Diane Roth, occupied a self-

contained basement suits in the Demers' house, where she
had lived for about three years. Mr. Demers was employed
as an installer/repairman for the B.C. Telephone Company,
which had employed him for 25 years. Carol-Ann was
a homemaker and a home-educator, as the Demers have
chosen to "home school" their children according to a
Christian education program.

Mr. Demers has been an extremely stable and law-abiding
citizen throughout his adult life. The only other trouble
with the law that he has experienced, occurred when he
was about 18 years old, when he tried to drive away from
a police car that had signaled him to stop. Mr. Demers
pleaded guilty to dangerous driving and he received a three-
month license suspension.

Mr. Demers does not have and adult (or childhood, or
adolescent) history of aggressive or violent behavior. To the
contrary, and as I will describe below, he has been a docile,
conciliatory, and slightly passive individual who eschews
aggressiveness. However, Mr. Demers had a slight altercation with Mr. Lee in April 1994, which did not result in
criminal charges for either party.

At the time of my assessment of Mr. Demers, he had been
in the community for 13 months, on bail, without negative
incident. Seemingly, he has scrupulously adhered to all of
his bail conditions. Apparently, the strain that has resulted
from this incident, and Mr. Demers ' current plight has
caused a temporary marital separation. Darwin is living
with his 19-year-old son David, in a Kelowna rental suite.
Coral-Ann and the other children are living in a suite, in
the Kelowna home of Dianne Roth. Mr. Demers is hopeful
and optimistic that he and Coral-Ann will reconcile. Mr.
Demers continues to be employed by B.C. Tel., although

he is not working in the cable maintenance and testing division.

RE: DEMERS Darwin
Page 3

Background Procedures

For the purposes of conducting this psychological assessment, I undertook a serious of extensive interviews with Mr. Demers. On February 11, I interviewed Mr. Demers for about two and three-quarter hours at his hotel. In addition, Mr. Demers completed the following psychological tests; the MMPI-2, the MCMI-2, the Stait Trait Anger Expression Inventory (STAXI) and the Exner Sentence Completion test. The interviews, psychological testing, and assessment in general were conducted with Mr. Demers' informed consent. Additionally, although Mr. Demers is at a pre-adjudication phase of legal proceedings, with his consent and upon my instruction, I discussed the particulars of this critical incident with him.

In addition to the foregoing procedures, my impressions and feelings have been informed by my review of a number of documents that you have sent to me. The documents included the Information, the police report to Crown Counsel (Narrative), and the transcripts and audiotapes of police interviews with Mr. Demers on January 2 and 4, 1995.

With respect to my qualifications, I have been frequently qualified as an expert witness in clinical and forensic psychology in the Supreme and Provincial Courts of B.C., as well as other jurisdictions, including Alberta,

Newfoundland, the Yukon and the North West Territories. In particular, I have considerable experience in the assessment and treatment of violent offenders. I enclose a concise summary of education, training and current clinical and consulting activities.

<u>Behavioral Observations and Impressions</u>

Mr. Demers appeared for the interviews as a neatly groomed man, with a boyish face and manner, which perhaps made him appear younger than his chronological age. He is of average height, and slightly portly build.

During the interview, Mr. Demers was well spoken. He possess an excellent vocabulary. He is quite loquacious, and he has a detailed approach to things. Mr. Demers

RE: DEMERS Darwin
Page 4

was exceedingly polite and deferential. He was very cooperative with all aspects of the evaluation. I believe that he is extremely respectful towards others Mr. Demers posses naturally good interpersonal skills. He likes people. He is genuinely friendly, good natured and interactive. He displayed a self-deprecating wit.

Through both my contacts with him, I found Mr. Demers to be humble and self effacing. He has a wholesome and "folksy" style, such that he is naturally prone to expressions, such as "By Golly!". At not time, did Mr. Demers express even the slightest profanity, even culturally accepted ones. Mr. Demers impressed me as a devout religious person, who possess so-called "traditional values", such as devotion to one's family, community and country, as well as a strong work ethic and moral conscience. Mr. Demers appears to be a very considerate and helpful person. In no way was it my impression that these qualities were feigned or otherwise self-serving.

During our interviews, Mr. Demers displayed a wide-range of emotions, that were appropriate to the context of our discussion. For example, he expressed much affection for his wife, children, and parent. He became teary-eyed and cried when we discussed the shooting of Mr. Lee and the impact of that event upon Mr. Demers ' wife, family and subsequent life. Mr. Demers was most distraught and sobbed uncontrollably when we discussed his history of conflict with Mr. Lee, and Mr. Demers is an ordinarily enthusiastic and optimistic person, despite his attempts to be upbeat in mood during our interviews, it was obvious that he is experiencing much emotional distress and his underlying dysphoria was made evident at many points in the interviews. Mr. Demers became very emotionally aroused during his recounting of his conflict with Mr. Lee, as if he was reliving some of those events and the feelings attached to them. At no time did Mr. Demers express hostility towards his victim. Mr. Demers was non-blaming of Mr. Lee and he (Darwin) took personal responsibility for his violent act, even though he does not believe that he was in control of his actions. I have no doubt that Mr. Demers deeply regrets his actions, and that he experiences empathy for Mr. Lee and his family, even though Mr. Lee caused Mr. Demers' great frustration.

In most forensic cases, the individual's mental state is usually det3ermined with heavy reliance on the individual's account, and the clinician's appraisal of the individual's veracity. I found Mr. Demers to be consistent in his account across our two interviews, as well as

RE: DEMERS Darwin
Page 5

With respect to what he has described to the police in their interviews. I perceived Mr. Demers to be open, candid and on-defensive. It was my impression that he was reporting life events and recalling the shooting incident to the best of his conscious ability. Mr. Demers provided thoughtful extensive answers to my questions.

On the basis of Mr. Demers' though and speech processes, I would estimate that he is of at least, above average intelligence. Although I did not formally assess it, Mr. Demers' memory is excellent in general, although it is spotty for many aspects of his experience associated with the critical incident that has given rise to his current charge. As I have noted above, Mr. Demers has excellent language skills, as well as a wide-ranging general knowledge.

Relevant Personal History

Mr. Demers was born in Meadow Lake, Saskatchewan, and he was raised predominately in Prince Albert, which has "produced three great Prime Ministers and was the home of John George Diefenbaker," according to Mr. Demers. As an 18-year-old, in the spring of 1965, Mr. Demers left home, and moved to Prince George, as a single man. After about a year or so, Mr. Demers returned to Prince Albert, as his relationship with Carol-Ann was "getting serious". After two more years in Saskatchewan, Mr. Demers returned to B.C. He and Carol-Ann were married in Kitimat. The have lived in B.D. since, apart from about two and one-half years spent in Saskatchewan in the late 1970s, when Mr. Demers and his brother-in-law undertook a private venture in the egg production business. Apart from that entrepreneurial endeavor, Mr. Demers has been employed by either Saskatchewan or B.C. telephone companies since his late teens. Around 1980, Mr. Demers and his family moved to Westbank, where the critical incident occurred.

Darwin's father worked as a plumber during Darwin's childhood and adolescence, although Darwin acknowledged that he preferred to remember his father "more romantically" as an air force veteran. Also, Darwin acknowledged that his father "drank too much" and that for a period of time, he owned and operated a hotel (in Meadow Lake), which according to Darwin "fit well" with his father's drinking habit. Darwin's mother occasionally worked part-time as a waitress.

RE: DEMERS Darwin
Page 6

Darwin described his parent in positive terms, and her remember them fondly, although he acknowledges that he wished that his father had drank less, when Darwin was a child. Darwin states that his father was sociable and popular with other people, when he was drinking. Darwin stated that his father was never verbally or physically abusive to him. Darwin says that his relationship with his father greatly improved over the last `5 years of his father's life, as his alcohol consumption had greatly diminished and he became "a great grandfather" for Darwin's children. Darwin's father died about six years ago, as a result of throat cancer. Darwin describes his father's illness, deterioration, and death as a disturbing experience for him (e.g., Darwin). About two years after Darwin's father died, Darwin's mother passed away as a result of cancer too.

Darwin expressed a near reverential attitude towards his mother, whom he greatly admired for keeping the family together, and tolerating her husband's alcohol abuse. Darwin states that his mother was good natured, sociable and popular as well, but in addition, she was a very responsible and well organized person. Darwin states that there was no doubt that his parent loved one another, and understandably, their relationship improved as Darwin's father's drinking diminished, particularly after they moved to B.C. in the 1970s, and Mr. Demers Sr. secured stable and well paying employment at various B.C. hydroelectric projects. Darwin states that there was never any undue conflict of violence between his parents, and although his father's alcohol abuse strained the family atmosphere, by and large, it was a happy and close one. Darwin is the eldest of three children. All of them are well adjusted, and they have experiences no social maladjustment. Darwin states that the family did not experience any undue trauma.

Darwin described his childhood personality as an "exuberant" and "extroverted" one. He believes that he was active, sociable, and "very outgoing". He states that he tried to please others, and that he was very sensitive to the needs of other people. In my opinion, these characteristics are very much still in evidence. During Darwin's adolescence, he continued to be an energetic teen. He was active in rodeo, and he had modest success in rock and roll bands. He continued to play music semi-professionally into his young adulthood.

Mr. Demers does not believe that he had any behavioral, emotional, or social problems during his childhood or adolescence. He was not aggressive or oppositional. He recounts only one fight during his childhood or adolescence, and as he describes it, it was a most benign one. Seemingly, Darwin's greatest childhood or adolescent act of misconduct occurred when he was 16 years old. He and a friend took Darwin's father's car, without

RE: DEMERS Darwin
Page 7

Permission, and drove into the Northern United States, with a vague idea of finding work on a dude ranch. They were pulled over in a routine check by highway patrol officers, and eventually, they were escorted home by Darwin's father ("none to pleased") as Darwin recalls. Darwin states that he has never experienced psychological, physical, or sexual abuse during his childhood or adolescence. In summary, Darwin appears to have been a well adjusted, stable, and happy child and adolescent.

On the educational front, Darwin states that he was "an under achiever", in that he believes that he did not attain grades that were comparable to intellectual abilities. He never failed any grades, but he characterizes himself as simply a below average student, whereas he (quite rightly) believes that he was likely capable of higher achievement. Darwin states that he was a slightly indifferent student, particularly during his adolescence, when he became quite interested in "rock and roll and girls". He says that he was something of a "class clown", although he was never suspended or expelled, andit seems that his classroom misconduct was probably quite mild. Mr. Demers does not have any post-high school education, apart from completing telecommunication courses, that were related to his work. However, he states that he "reads alot". I found his general knowledge and vocabulary to be quite impressive. In addition, as an adult, Mr. Demers has conducted bible studies for his church parish.

Vocationally, Mr. Demers has demonstrated a very stable and successful working history, as well as a strong work ethic. During his adolescence, he routinely held part-time jobs in retail stores, or animal-care, as he loved horses and animals in general. Mr. Demers' first full-time job occurred when he was 18 years old, when he was employed by B.C. Tel., and by and large, he has worked for telephone companies, either in B.C. or Saskatchewan since. Mr. Demers discontinued his involvement with rock bands, in his early twenties, as he was distressed by "the appearance of drugs in the music scene": He was strongly opposed to drug use. He decided to discontinue performing music as a result.

As mentioned above, in the late 1970s, Mr. Demers joined his brother-in-law, is a Saskatchewan egg production business. At that time, Mr. Demers had become slightly dissatisfied with his telephone company job as there appeared to be no opportunities for advancement. As well, he, Carol-Ann and their family had been living in Dawson Creek for about 12 years, and they thought it might be time to "move on". According to Mr. Demers, he found the private enterprise to be overly demanding of his time, and he was

Re: DEMERS Darwin
Page 8

unhappy that it did not permit him to spend more time with
his family. Mr. Demers recognized that he did not have
an entrepreneurial temperament, or strong materialistic
desires. He and his family decided to return to B.C., where
he resumed his work with the telephone company, which
continues to the present day.

Although Mr. Demers has a history of slight head injuries,
it would not appear that any of these was serious enough to
influence his personal adjustment, or to contribute in any
way to the critical incident which brings Mr. Demers into
the criminal justice system now. Mr. Demers has not had
previous contact with mental health professionals. He does
not abuse alcohol or drugs.

Seemly, throughout Mr. Demers' life, he has established
good to excellent interpersonal relationships. He has made
friends easily, and kept them. He dated extensively in his
adolescence and early adulthood. He believes that he was
popular with girls, particularly one he became involved in
rock bands. Mr. Demers has a very positive and respectful
attitude towards women. In fact, he tends to be quite ideal-
izing of them. He has formed strong attachments to women.
He has been quite dependent on the significant women in
his life, particularly his wife and his mother. He strongly
values a mother's role in the family and home. According
to Mr. Demers, he and his wife have enjoyed an excellent
marriage, until the last year, when the stress associated with
Mr. Demers' current plight prompted separation. As well,
Mr. Demers does recognize that his marital relationship was
strained, due to the conflict which was occurring with their
neighbors, the Lee family. Mr. Demers was guilt-ridden

that he was not more assertive or effective in protecting his family, particularly his wife, from the rudeness and abuse that was directed at her by Steven Lee. Mr. Demers states that he and his wife began arguing more in the last couple of years, as the conflicts with their neighbor intensified.

THE HISTORY AND NATURE OF THE RELATIONSHIP BETWEEN MR. DEMERS AND MR LEE

According to Mr. Demers, the Lee family moved next door in the spring of 1992. The initial conflicts between the neighbors and Mr. Lee's complaints to Mr. Demers focused primarily on Mr. Demers' children, especially his teenage son, David. Mr. Demers states that Mr. Lee would commonly sear at Darwin's children and wife (e.g., "Yo Bitch! Yo Slut!") and make obscene gestures towards them. As well, Mr. Lee would make animal noises, such as grunting or oinking, presumably to represent his attitude that he considered

RE: Demers Darwin
Page 9

The Demers family members to be pigs. During the second year of the relationship, Mr. Demers states that Mr. Lee's focus shifted towards him, although Mr. Lee continued to make rude comments and noises as well as obscene gestures towards Darwin's wife and children. During the second year of the conflict, Mr. Lee thrice reports that Mr. Demers had an illegal suite and tenant in his home, and those reports generated inspections and financial costs for Mr. Demers as he was required to modify the suite.

In the third year of Mr. Demers' and Mr. Lee's relationship, Mr. Demers states that he was increasingly harassed by Mr. Demers. For example, Mr. Demers says that Mr. Lee reported him for having an illegal fire and fire trucks were dispatched. On three occasions, Mr. Demers' employer was called, and a citizen (who Mr. Demers believe to have been Mr. Lee) reported that Mr. Demers had a company service truck at his home. In April of 1994, Mr. Lee and Mr. Demers came to blows, and their brief altercation appears to have been triggered by Mr. Lee's resentment and anger about Mr. Demers planting a cedar hedge which separated and screened the Lee and Demers' properties. According to Mr. Demers, during the altercation, Mr. Lee ordered his boxer dog to attack Mr. Demers. Mr. Demers states that in the past Mr. Lee threatened to have his dog attack the Demers children.

In the aftermath of the April 1994 fight, Mr. Demers recognized that all of his attempts to peacefully co-exist with his neighbor had failed, and Darwin reached the difficult decision to sell his home. He was sickened by the prospect of moving, as he had considered the house and neighbor hood ideal. As well, his parents had lived in that home for the least ten years for their lives, and for that reason and many more, Mr. Demers was strongly attached to his home and neighborhood, which he now decided to forsake. However, the real estate market was poor, and the Demers had difficulty selling their home, such that Mr. Demers felt increasingly trapped. As well over the course of his conflict with Mr. Lee, Mr. Demers (and his family) had experienced property damage and theft, which Mr. Demers attributed to Mr. Lee. For example, Mr. Demers installed an automatic, underground sprinkling system, and many times, his sprinkler heads were broke. He had a large hose stolen. Oftentimes, his son's newspaper bundles were taken in the morning. Mr. Demers had a new truck vandalized, as its doors were scraped. Mr. Demers' son had gravel and scratches put on his car's roof. Mr. Demers attributed these malicious actions to Mr. Lee.

RE: DEMERS Darwin
Page 10

Mr. Demers claims that he and his family were frequently threatened by Mr. Lee. Apart from Mr. Lee pretending to release his dog and having it attack, Mr. Demers told me that Mr. Lee threatened to blow up the Demers' house and to "pick off" or shoot various members of the Demers family. This latter threat was often accompanied by Mr. Lee's "gun drills" (Mr. Demers' words) and other sorts of para-military actions that Mr. Lee performed in front of the Demers family.

If Mr. Demers' description is accurate, Mr. Lee seems to be a volatile, hostile, immature, confrontational and aggressive person. Given my impression of Mr. Lee, as described by Mr. Demers , Mr. Lee seems to be the classic bully, in that he is cruel, threatening, and taunting.

I accept as given that Mr. Demers made a concerted attempt to avoid conflict with Mr. Lee, but Darwin states that he and his family experienced ceaseless torment, by virtue of more or less constant provocation and harassment. I have no doubt that Mr. Demers experienced a psychological state of intimidation, fear, emasculation, impotency, helplessness and suppressed anger. Mr. Demers' self respect also dimin-ished, as he became more socially withdrawn at home, and to some extent homebound in the neighborhood as he endeavored to avoid any kind of interactions with Mr. Lee.

I believe that Mr. Demers became quite depressed in the latter part of 1994. The psychological state that Mr. Demers experienced as a result of Mr. Lee's abuses comparable to that experienced by a battered spouse. Quite accurately, Mr. Demers can be called a psychologically battered neighbor.

DEFENDANT'S ACCOUNT OF THE CRITICAL INCIDENT

Mr. Demers does not recall any undue frustrations or stressors earlier in the day on which he shot Mr. Lee. Mr. Demers believes that his aggression towards Mr. Lee was initially triggered by overhearing his wife remark to their friend that Mr. Lee was making obscene and threatening gestures towards her. At that point, it appears that Mr. Demers experienced a state of psychological dissociation, such that his conscious mind was disconnected from his body and actions. From that moment on, he became a bystander to, and witness of his actions, rather than the conscious director of them. Mr. Demers describes

RE: DEMERS Darwin
Page 11

himself as experiencing a dialogue between his good and bad selves, which were directing him to choose between good and bad actions. Mr. Demers' own words are most apt. In the immediate aftermath of hearing his wife's remarks about Mr. Lee's rudeness, Mr. Demers believes that his "brain shifted right then...my brain shifted into a conversation with itself". Mr. Demers reports that that dialogue continued throughout his interaction with, and the shooting of Mr. Lee. However, Mr. Demers does not believe that he was an active agent, who was consciously guiding his behaviors. Mr. Demers told me, "my body became the servant of whoever was going to win the argument...I'm like a third person listening to both sides of the conversation".

Mr. Demers describes his mental state and psychological experience in a fashion that is consistent with an extreme degree of depersonalization, in that he felt very detached from his own experience as if he was an outside observer of his thoughts and behaviors. Again, Mr. Demers' own words are most descriptive of this experience. He said "I could look at my body and see it reacting as cool as a cucumber...as if I was behind it...but it was my brain" or "I'm following, watching myself go back up the hall" or "my eyes are watching this and sending back information". Each of these comments reflects the extent to which Mr. Demers was in the psychological role of a bystander or observer of his own body, behaviors and mental processes. In short, it doesn't seem that Mr. Demers had a conscious, self directed sense of determining his own actions. For example, he said, "the gun goes up to my shoulder", reflecting the extent to which his actions seemed disembodied. Additionally, Mr. Demers described experiences of de-realization, which is an experience of feeling as if in a dream, as if things are not real. He stated, "I did not want the whole things to be happening...I kept saying to myself this isn't happening...its like a dream". Mr. Demers states that he has no conscious recall for many events or actions, which others have said occurred. For example, Mr. Demers knows that member of his family have said that he came back into the house after the shooting, before going into the woods. Seemingly, an amnesia exists for that event, as well as other aspects of Mr. Demers' experience. He does not believe that he re-entered the house (even though he does not recall it), and he believes that the witnesses are wrong. After Mr. Demers was arrested, his consciousness continues to seem somewhat disturbed, while he was in police custody and during the police interviews.

RE: DEMERS Darwin
Page 12

OPINION AND RECOMMENDATIONS

Mr. Demers is a conservative, conventional man, who holds so-called "traditional values": He is religious, national-istic, law-abiding, considerate, respectful of authority, as well as protective and supportive of his wife and children. Throughout Mr. Demers' life he has been stable and well adjusted. There are slight dependent and compulsive traits in his personality, but these are not pathological. However, control of one's self and one's emotion is important to Mr. Demers. Mr. Demers does not have a psychological disorder, present or past. He is not antisocial. He does not have a criminal value system. To the contrary, he is extremely moral and honest. Interpersonally, he is not an aggressive person. To the contrary, he is friendly, gregar-ious and slightly passive. He has not been an assaultive or violent person throughout his life, withstanding the events that prompted his current charge.

As a result of the conflicts with Mr. Lee, I believe that Mr. Demers developed a psychological state, that is comparable to that which is often seen in battered spouses. In my view, Mr. Demers was depressed, fearful and hopeless. Primarily, he coped with the conflict with Mr. Lee through passive resignation, avoidance and withdrawal.

At the time Mr. Demers shot Mr. Lee, I believe that Mr. Demers was in an altered state of consciousness. I believe that he was in a state of psychological dissociation. Dissociation is a psychological term that refers to the profound disruption in the normally integrated thoughts, feelings, and behaviors of a person. In a dissociative state, a person is not consciously aware of his behaviors, and he is not in cognitive control of his actions. While experiencing a dissociative state, the individual does not have a normal awareness of his actions. Nor is he able to anticipate the normal consequences of those actions, or to evaluate his conduct and seek alternative ways of behaving. Ordinarily, dissociative states occur in times of great emotional stress, and may be prompted by a significant psychological stressor. In Mr. Demers' case, in my view, the precipitating even which led to his dissociation was overhearing and learning that Mr. Lee had made obscene and aggressive gestures towards Mr. Demers' wife.

From that time on, Mr. Demers appears to be psychologically disconnected from his actions, such that, in my opinion, his violent actions towards Mr. Lee were automatic,

RE: DEMERS Darwin
Page 13

Involuntary ones. Again I found Mr. Demers' own words to be most telling of his experience. He said to me "something were happening in spite of what I wanted to happen", referencing the extent to which he felt like a bystander or observer of his own conduct, rather than the director of it.

In a case of this kind, one must obviously try and determine the extent to which Mr. Demers' behavior and experience is most accurately characterized as one of dissociation, as opposed to simply an extreme loss of temper, with associated violent behavior. In my opinion, the former psychological explanation is more tenable. I believe that Mr. Demers' mental state and experience is most consistent with his being in a dissociative state. His conduct is most atypical for him. He has only a vague or patchy recollection for some of his actions, and other actions he made are seemingly not consciously available to him. There is no evidence of premeditation for the critical incident. Mr. Demers does not have a conscious experience of being enraged or angry during the course of the events that culminated in the shooting of Mr. Lee. In the aftermath of the shooting, Mr. Demers' behavior is consistent with that of an individual who is greatly distressed by what he has done. His emotional crisis is much in evidence during the police interviews. In fact, Mr. Demers' consciousness still seems to be somewhat clouded and confused after the event, inasmuch, as during the first police interview, he could not remember his wife's first name or the ages of his children. During the period of dissociation, Mr. Demers had a number of psychological experiences that are typical of dissociation, including feelings of depersonalization (e.g., "my hand grabs the gun"), time sense distortion, and even some visual distortions, such as the perception that the gun barrel was lengthening.

In my view, Mr. Demers most likely has suffered considerably because of his actions. He is ashamed of his violent behavior. His once solid marriage, home and family life have been destabilized and become quite tenuous. Obviously, there has been considerable financial costs to his as well, by virtue of his involvement with the criminal justice system. Regardless of the outcome of Mr. Demers' trial, I believe that he would benefit from a period of therapy or counseling that was oriented towards him in better coping with the guilt that he experiences for his wrongdoing as well as to better cope with his stressful life circumstance.

RE: DEMERS Darwin
Page 14

These then are my impressions, findings, and recommendations. I trust that this information will increase your understanding of your client. I appreciate your seeking my consultation in this most interesting, but tragic case.

Sincerely,

Robert G. Ley, Ph.D.
Clinical and Consulting Psychologist

RGL/a

Dr. S. Lohrasbe, Inc
ADULT PSYCHIATRY

Mailing Address: P.O. Box 2010 Sidney, B.C. V8L 3S3 • Office: Suite #3 - 1517 Amelia Street, Victoria, B.C.
Telephone 360-3040

26 March 1996

BRIEF CURRICULUM VITAE

Forensic Psychiatric Experience:

Sessional employment since 1985 with the Forensic Psychiatric Services Commission. Between 1985 and September 1992, worked at the Forensic Psychiatric Institute in Port Coquitlam, providing assessment and treatment to the mentally disordered. Since September 1992 am based at the Victoria Out-patient Clinic of Forensic Psychiatric Services, and provide consultations to the Vancouver Island Regional Correction Centre.

I have testified at all levels of trial Courts in B.C., the Yukon and the North West Territories. I also provide Psychiatric Assessments for the National Parole Board.

To date I have assessed more than 3000 individuals charged or convicted for a criminal offence. I have testified in Court about 300 times, and have taken part in more than one dozen Dangerous Offender proceedings.

I have extensive experiences in Forensic Psychiatry, especially issues around the assessment of violent offenders, sexual offenders, substance-abusing offenders and a full range of mentally disordered offenders. Specific issues often addressed include mental state at time f offense, fitness for trial, general case management and future risk to community.

General Psychiatric Experience:

Director of in-patient Psychiatric Unit at Yarmouth
Regional Hospital (Nova Scotia) 1984-1985. Currently,
small general private practice.

Qualifications:

Basic Medical training in India, 1978. Subsequent qualifying examinations in Canada.

Residency in Psychiatry at UBC (1980-1984). Chief
Resident, 1983. Sic months of specific training in Forensic
Psychiatry, 1984. Passes fellowship exams at end of
Residency and have been a fellow of the Royal College of
Physicians and Surgeons of Canada since 1984. Fully quali-
fied to practice Medicine in B.C.

Dear Mr. Jackson,

RE: Darwin Demers
D.O.B. 22 January 1947

The following is a summary of my psychiatric opinion in
regards to Mr. Demers' mental state during the incident of
02 January 1995. Please accept my profuse apology for the
delay in getting this report to you.

For the preparation for this report I interview Mr. Demers
in Vancouver for approximately two and one half hours
on the 10 February 1996. I also reviewed the documenta-
tion that you made available to me including the relevant

police report, two police interviews with Mr. Demers, a
brief psychiatric report written by Dr. Stanly Semrau dated
03 January 1995 and your covering letter to me dated 15
January, 24 January and 14 March 1996. I understand
that Mr. Demers has been psychologically assessed by Br.
Robert Ley but as of yet I have not had the opportunity to
review Dr. Ley's report.

At the outset of my interview with Mr. Demers, he was
made aware of the purpose of the assessment, its limited
confidentiality, and his right to refuse to discuss anything
he did not wish to. He was made aware that although I was
retained by you on his behalf, I was obligated to provide a
neutral and objective assessment.

Background

Although I took a detailed personal history from Mr.
Demers, Will not explore it in this report as I understand
that you will be bringing forth that history in Court. From
a psychiatric perspective, the relevant features are negative, i.e. no serious medical behavioral or emotional problems until the onset of the circumstances leading up to the
shooting. Mr. Demers had no prior psychiatric history.

Mental State Examination

When interview, Mr. Demers presented as a pleasant, spon-
taneous and talkative individual with a very easy going
manner. He did become tense, anxious and tearful at several
points when describing the very stressful experiences he
and his family endured in the last three years or so before
the shooting. He also w2as quite tearful when discussing
his worries about his children's future and how it has been
implicated by his own actions.

Despite his understandably high level of anxiety and concern about his family's future, Mr. Demers does not currently suffer from a depressive syndrome. There are some depressive themes, centered around helplessness, shame and guilt. However, he states that his mood is no persistently low and that with the passing of time he has gained some perspective and hop around his situation. He is not currently suicidal.

Mr. Demers does not describe any of the features associated with a psychiatric disorder of psychotic proportions. For instance, there is no evidence of hallucinations or other perceptual symptoms, paranoia or other types of delusions or any gross disorder in thinking. He was fully oriented, was able top focus his attention on the topic under consideration, and spoke on a range of issues in a coherent and goal directed manner.

I found Mr. Demers to be a very credible individual. His personal history is very suggestive of this as is his ingenuous clinical presentation. I got the very strong sense that he was an honest man with considerable personal integrity.

<u>Circumstances Leading Up to the Offense</u>

Here again it is my understanding that you will be leading detailed evidence about the horrific circumstances that Mr. Demers and his family were exposed to as a result of the action of their neighbor, the victim of the shooting. From a psychiatric point of view what is important to note is that the strain had continued for more than two and half years and Mr. Demers' repeated attempts at pacifying his neighbor and later, tolerating the various forms of abuse had all led nowhere. He was under siege in his own home and was fearful for his safety and the safety of his family. Over time, he became significantly depressed and described himself as a changed man. He became irritable, sad, and withdrew from social interaction. The chronic sense of tension and anxiety undercut his usual interests and pastimes. He describes a profound sense of helplessness after repeated attempts at resolving some of the difficulties were unsuccessful. In the late summer of 1994 he placed his home on the market in order to get away from the neighbor but even this drastic step (he had lived happily in the home for more than 12 years before the neighbor moved in) left him unsure as to whether he could actually escape the strain, as he was given to believe that moving away would still leave him vulnerable to the neighbor, Steven Lee.

It was against this background that the incident itself occurred. His recall of the exact circumstances is patchy. What is striking is the speed with which the incident evolved and the lack of any obvious and immediate build-up. At about 4:30 in the afternoon on the 2nd of January 1995, Mr. Demers was watching the Canadian Junior Hockey Team win a tournament and was in good spirits. Heading from the family room to the kitchen he heard his wife Carol tell their friend and houseguest that Mr. Lee had just "given the finger and called her names". He recalls hearing words to that effect and recalls no particular thought content connecting those words and his subsequent actions. He turned the corner, opened a closet door, grabbed a 12 gauge shotgun and some shells from the shelf and "I took the gun and the shells up around the turn around. While this is going on I'm thinking, this is not happening, please this is not happening. All I heard, 50-60 feet away, all I heard was 'you're in trouble now'. I heard nothing else and saw nothing else. He's walking towards me, with wheelbarrow full of stuff. I had my gun. I remember 'bang,' remember having it go bang and looking and seeing that nothing happened. He didn't fall, nothing, no blood."

Following the shooting, he recalls that he felt "all disjointed, all jumbled up." He could not think clear and he felt detached, as though in a dream. He subsequently made an effort to shoot himself by putting the shotgun into his mouth. After he found that this was difficult to do, he sat and gradually "I started to return to a calm, complacent state and realized that what had happened and that suicide wouldn't help."

Opinion

A current mental state examination as well as a review of Mr. Demers' background reveals no evidence of a major psychiatric disorder. However, the history suggests that he was depressed in mood prior to the shooting and that at the time of the shooting itself he experienced the process of mental dissociation.

This process, a "dissociative state", can occur under a variety of circumstances and manifest in different ways. The word dissociation refers to a disruption in mental cohesion and functioning, so that some aspect of ongoing mental functioning are broken off, or dissociated, from the others.

Normal mental function requires the coordination of several mental processes simultaneously so that the individual perceives his reality accurately, makes meaningful connections, generates appropriate choices and acts on them on the basis of his needs and desires. When there is a gross disruption in the integration of these processes - a dissociation - the individual is not functioning as coherent, rational individual. Instead, one or more mental processes, functioning independently, generate actions that are not in accord with the individual's overall desires, plans or intentions. Such a conceptualization is necessarily theoretical (it cannot be concretely demonstrated) but has long and well accepted genealogy within psychiatry.

In order to diagnose a state of dissociation during the incident, as against simple anger, I considered several issues. Starting with his history, it is apparent that he is not an impulsive or aggressive individual and I will leave it to you to show in great detail the very contrary. Also important is his credibility which hinges on whether you believe his account. I do.

Next we come to the situation itself. It is well recognized that dissociative episodes are far more likely to occur under conditions of extreme stress. For instance, they are seen very frequently after trauma such as war, earthquakes, sexual assaults, etc... Also, individuals can be primed for a dissociative episode through a gradual alteration of their mental state away from their normal, coordinated, coherent functioning. Such did happen with Mr. Demers as he became progressively anxious and depressed.

Further clues that he was in a dissociative state are embedded in his account of the incident itself. His memory is patchy, which is often the case. He reports one part of his observant self being separated from and struggling with his acting self. Such depersonalization is a frequent accompaniment of dissociation. Also frequent is the kind of dual consciousness that he reports. He also reports a limited and selective focusing in some aspects of his immediate environment with neglect of others. This is also common in dissociation.

Keep in mind also the abrupt onset of his actions. One minute he is in a good mood and cheering Canada onto victory, the next he is loading his shotgun. Such an abrupt onset also is consistent with dissociation. He also reports some discrepancy between what he recalls doing and what his wife subsequently told him he did do. Again, this supports dissociation.

None of these features, taken alone, can ensure the diagnosis. Taken together and put in to the context of Mr. Demers' personality and history, they are compelling.

There is no specific link between the clinical diagnosis or a dissociative episode and any specific legal finding. If, for instance, Mr. Demers had a history of a major psychiatric disorder such as schizophrenia then such a description of his mental state during an incident may provide psychiatric support for finding of Not Criminally Responsible by Reason of Mental Disorder. However, Mr. Demers has no such psychiatric history. As best as I understand the fit between psychiatric findings and the law, I believe that my opinion will more closely match the legal finding of Non Insane Automatism.

Thank you for asking me to assess Mr. Demers. Feel free to give me a call if you have any questions about this report.

Sincerely,

S. Lohrasbe, MBBS, FRCPC
Psychiatrist

Memorandum

To: Ritchie Clark
From: D Michael Bain
Date: August 8, 1996
Re: Summary of testimony from criminal trial concerning
mental state of Darwin David DEMERS in shooting of
Stephen Barry LEE.

Brief Summary

On Friday, July 19, 1996, in the Supreme Court of British
Columbia, Darwin David Demers was acquitted by jury
of all criminal charges stemming from a shooting incident
which took place on January 2, 1995 near Kelowna B.C.
Stephen Lee was shot three times by a shotgun loaded
with bird shot causing injuries to his upper right chest, left
arm and left leg. The acquittal of Darwin Demers from the
charges of attempted murder and discharging a firearm with
the intent to wound main or disfigure arose from psychiatric
evidence raised at trial as to Demers' state of mind at the
time of the shooting incident. Demers' psychiatric condition
is best understood in the context of having suffered several
years of harassment and threats from Mr. Lee. Evidence as
to his mental state came from Darwin Demers' own testimony as well as testimony from Br. Shadarand Lohrasbe,
a forensic psychiatrist, and Dr. Robert Ley, a clinical and
forensic psychologist. Both doctors testified that at the time
of the incident Mr. Demers was in a dissociative state and
was not therefore in conscious control of his actions.

Testimony of Darwin David Demers

Darwin Demers was called as a witness for the defense
and gave his testimony on Tuesday, July 16, 1996. In chief
examination Demers testified that the situation between he
and Mr. Lee had deteriorated almost from the moment Lee
moved in next door to the Demers family. He said that he
felt that the situation was serious from the outset as they
were unable to find a way to peacefully co-exist with one
another. Demers recounted a number of incidents of threats
made by Lee towards Demers and his family as well as a
fist fight that had taken place between the two men. These
incidents, particularly the ones involving threats to his wife
and children, left Demers feeling scared for the safety of
his family and confused over Lee's often bizarre actions.
During testimony, Demers stated: "I don't understand that.
There's something wrong with that man."

Because of Lee's behavior and the constant threats, Demers
eventually put his house up for sale although he did not
want to leave as he had put so much work into the house
and described it as "a part of me" since both his parents
had died there. Yet Demers knew Lee was not going to
move himself and it was because of Lee that Demers' wife,
Carol, "was a nervous wreck." Demers testified that he
did not want to move, that he "had to move…I gave up.
Family comes first. Life on this planet is too short. We had
to leave." Demers also noted that he became withdrawn,
spent most of his time inside, fixed sprinklers in the dark so
as not to aggravate the foul-mouthed neighbor, and spent
most of his time in the television room. "To my shame I
wouldn't go out on the deck," he stated, "I spent $11,000
to fix the deck up then didn't use it." The death threats
especially seared Demers, but his chief concern was for
his wife, Carol, who was "really shook up [sic]." Demers

wanted to think "none of this [was] happening," but he also
testified that "if you are told your house will be blown up,
you do sleep with one eye open...I thought we might not
make it through the night." Demers even described himself
as feeling "crackerjacks [or] nutty" as a result of constant
harassment from Lee.

Describing the day of the incident, Demers noted that he
had spent the day watching a junior hockey game with his
son, David. Since Canada won the game he felt "euphoric,
happy, intoxicated with excitement." As he came down
the hall with his coffee cup, Demers heard his wife, Carol,
telling her friend that she had "just got the finger and the
fist from Lee." Demers then stated "my mind snapped,
I experienced nutiness [sic], craziness." At that point a
conversation began in Demers' mind between a dominant and passive self, Demers testified: "I became and
observer...a passive recorder of events. My body became
the servant of the dominant side." When asked about his
use of the word "observer," Demers stated that it was his
own word meaning that he was "just along for the ride." If
one analyzed the situation, according to Demers, one might
use the word "detached," but it is not a word he would use
himself. Instead Demers describes his experience as "not
consciously directing my thoughts, just recording them."

Demers knows he grabbed the gun, some shells, his coat
and boots before leaving the house, but referring to his
mental condition explained that he had "never experienced
anything like it." He described a real conversation going on
in his brain as if actual voices were talking and that he was
"taken kicking and creaming up that hill." One side was
asking "why take ammo?' the other side was saying "this
has got to look good." Demers said his passive side was
thinking "this is illegal, immoral, wrong" but that when he

saw Lee, lee gave him the finger and said "you're in trouble now" causing him confusion over why Lee did not seem to be at all scared.

At this point Demers' testimony became fragmented and he testified "up goes the gun...bang! We come close to one another face to face, whether I hit him with the gun or he walked into it, I don't know. We stood there for 5 - 10 second face to face. Frozen. It seemed like a long time. There was lots of time for me to record what was going on. What's going on, what's happening? The dominant side says 'he's scared, keep him running.' Band! I take off running. I understand that he took off and turned around...'keep him running' Bang!" Next, Demers grabbed his jacket and more ammunition from his front deck (his memory is confused here as his testimony conflicts with his son, David, and his wife, Carol, who both testified that they saw him in the front hallway after the shooting). Demers says he went into the woods where he tried to put the gun in his mouth but the barrel seemed to get "longer, longer, longer." According to Demers, he might not have really wanted to kill himself and he now thinks that it was perhaps a feeble attempt at suicide. He saw his son, Mark, coming into the woods with a crowbar, but told him to home. Demers then fired the gun off, set the safety, leaned the gun against a tree and "waited for the panting of a (police) dog."

Demers recalled saying nothing at all during the incident and does not think he was in control of his actions. In fact, when asked whether he was consciously in control or not, he replied "I felt like an observer of what was happening the whole time. Two sides were fighting, one winning, one losing. The body was serving the winning side, I was just recording the sights and sounds." When asked what his

intentions were, Demers testified that the dominant side of
him told him not to shoot, just to scare Lee. Then the voise
was saying "'aim to the right, aim to the right'…which I
believe I did." The was no indication to Demers that Lee
had been hit and his dominant side was saying "see, there's
nothing to worry about, everything's going to be fine."
When Lee looked down the muzzle of the gun and moaned,
Demers says he thought "this worked, he's scared." Demers
categorically stated "I never wanted to kill anyone. I never
wanted to kill Mr. Lee. I only wanted him to leave my
family alone." Further, he testified that he "never wanted
to threaten lee, and never wanted to hurt him" Regarding
the second and third shots, Demers testified that eh did not
intend to hurt Lee, "my intention was to scare him and keep
him running." I wanted to scare him, keeping him funning,
tell him to leave my family alone."

On cross examination Demers testified that he felt that
because he had told the police verbally of the threats to his
family, he had no reason to phone them. He also stated that
he had no way of explaining that what was serious to him
and his family was apparently trivial to the police. During
the fist fight, for example, there had been no internal debate
in Demers' although he did feel a duty to go outside and
fight. Demers admitted to being highly frustrated with Lee
in general and emotionally excited just before the shooting
incident began. When asked what he was planning to do
with the gun Demers replied that he intended to scare
Mr. Lee. At various times throughout cross-examination,
Demers testified that he aimed to miss and intended to scare
Lee. Again, Demers described a "violent conversation that
erupted between a dominant and passive side," and that
he had "no conscious direction of [his] thoughts." Demers
described his body becoming the servant of the side
winning the conversation. The incident itself was "surre-

alistic" and according to Demers he was "not conscious mover of those thoughts or that body." Demers also testified that he did not know whether he had a nervous breakdown or temporary insanity...everything was bizarre and confused."

Testimony of Dr. R. Ley

During Demers' testimony, Dr. R. Ley was present in the court room and based his diagnosis in part on Demers' statements to the court which he found consistent with Demers' earlier statements. Dr. R. Ley's testimony was also based on over six hours of extensive interview he held with Mr. Demers on February 9, 1996 and February 11, 1996 as well as the following psychological tests, the MMPI-2, the MCMI-2, the Stait Trait Anger Expression Inventory (STAXI) and the Exner Sentence Completion test. A report based on those interviews and test was prepared by Dr. R. Ley for defense counsel and he referred to it in part during his testimony I court. Although Dr. R. Ley was aware that Dr, Lohrasbe was also assessing Demers, he did not discuss the patient with Lohrasbe or see his report before reaching his own conclusions. The court qualified Dr. R. Ley as an expert in clinical and forensic psychology and he gave his opinion on Tuesday, July 16, 1996.

Dr. R. Ley gave a general description of psychology to the court and noted that it is a broad discipline. He described that the focus in his own research and practice has been on the cognitive, social and developmental aspects of psychology. A distinction was made between clinical psychology, where the emphasis is on treatment, assessment and diagnosis of mental illnesses and forensic psychology, which looks at the interaction between psychology and the law. Dr. R. Ley recounted the methods he used to reach his diagnosis and noted that he also had copies of the police report to the Crown, audio tapes of

Demers' lengthy statements to the police and transcripts of the same.

The purpose of the first interview was for Dr. R. Ley to familiarize himself with Demers, to establish a rapport, and to collect a social, medical and criminal history. Dr. R. Ley was interested in a comprehensive picture of Demers' psychological development. Credibility is important in a forensic context as well as in reaching a diagnosis for treatment purposes; Dr. R. Ley believes Demers' reported things openly, candidly and freely. In determining the psychological makeup of Demers, Dr. R. Ley looked to Demers' own account of the incident, witness statement of what they observed and the subject's hisoty and behavioral characteristics. As there is a good deal of information on "faking" or malingering, Dr. R. Ley noted that it would be quite difficult for a subject to fake a condition. Moreover, the results of the written tests given to Demers were consistent with Dr. R. Ley's clinical impressions of Mr. Demers as a non-defensive individual.

Also consistent between the test results and clinical impression were the fact that Demers is a sociable, interactive and friendly individual who has traditional views and values based on a strong conviction in Christian morality and beliefs. Dr. R. Ley found Demers to be a rather traditional male who is normally not aggressive or anti-social with the present incident being the exception. There was a dependent trait in Demers' personality and tended to be submissive and passive rather than assertive. Demers also values and respects women with particular respect for his mother and his wife.

Demers was extremely emotional in recounting the events leading up to the shooting, crying frequently and sobbing uncontrollably in his interviews with Dr. R. Ley. It was clear to Dr. R. Ley that over the course of the conflict, Demers became passive, fearful and avoidant - entirely consistent with his personality traits. Under the stress of the relationship with Mr. Lee, Demers' passive qualities were emphasized. The decision not to phone the police about the various events was consistent with Demers' desire to avoid conflict or trouble. These was a "progressive isolation: to Demers' world experience as he went from being first reluctant to go into the neighborhood, then refused to go in his yard, then would no use his deck, finally would stay inside the house, then limited himself largely to using only the television room. Demers was essentially becoming a psychological prisoner in his own home somewhat akin to the condition of a battered spouse. Demers felt helpless, frustrated and ineffective and became a passive, psychologically battered neighbor.

Dr. R. Ley described Demers' mental state on January 2, 1995 as being one of psychological dissociation. The term dissociation is used to refer to situations where there is a profound disconnection between thoughts, feelings and actions. Whereas people are usually coherent, during dissociation there is a breakdown, division, or separation of thought processes and a lack of coherence. Dissociation occurs on a continuum from mild to sever, where mild might be a state of daydreaming and more sever would be highway hypnosis. Very severe forms of dissociation are much more rare such as sleepwalking or multiple personality disorder. The condition is most likely to occur under stressful circumstances and while there is debate in the scientific community, there is little debate regarding dissociation as a psychological phenomenon.

Dr. R. Ley's reasoning for diagnosing this condition in Demers are outlined below. First, it was otherwise not an unusual day. There were no particular frustrations although the conflict had been going on for some time. Demers was depressed and withdrawn, but when he heard the statement made but his wife concerning Lee's threatening gestures, a division took place in his mind between what Demers originally termed his "good and bad selves"; in his testimony in court he used the terms passive and dominant. The dialogue seemed to continue throughout the incident with Lee. After the final shot, the conversation concluded in the woods. Normally people do not have fully articulated conversations in their minds, Demers described the dialogues as intense, vivid and raging,.

Second, Demers described himself as not being an active agent. He was not consciously moving his body and described himself in the third person. Most clinicians refer to this condition as one of depersonalization. Demers was an observer of his thoughts and actions, rather than the director of them. He described his body being carried out the door, up the hill and onto the street, with anger there is not this type of disconnection. A person who is normally indecisive in his life does not experience this type of disconnection.

Third, there was a sense of de-realization where the experience did not seem real. Demers described the incident as being "surreal" and that he "did not want the whole thing to be happening." Demers watched himself performing and was confused regarding certain events. He couldn't recall certain things such as his wife's name when the police asked him. This is the fourth criteria Dr. R. Ley found to support a diagnosis of dissociation: a patchy memory, where the subject is cloudy or vague on certain details. Demers does not recall certain movements or statements. Amnesia or confusion is typical of dissociative conditions.

All of these incidents suggest to Dr. R. Ley that Demers' consciousness was disturbed. The fact that he was able to carry out complex actions is typical of people in dissociative conditions where they can appear quite normal but in reality they are not in conscious control of their action. To bystanders a dissociating subject can appear to perform goal directed or logical behavior. There can also be a gradual recovery of memory over time although scientifically this is difficult to determine as the condition is rare and not well documented in laboratory conditions. As far as Demers describing the barrel of the gun getting longer and longer Dr. R. Ley noted that dissociating subjects often experience disturbances in their sensory observations such that things appear to sound different. This perhaps explains why Demers did not hear himself say anything if he did, in fact, speak to Lee during the shooting. Dr. R. Ley believes that the dissociative state began to phase out while Demers was in the woods. He concluded that Demers, in a dissociative state, did not behave voluntarily and did not direct his actions. He further stated that Demers' consciousness was severely impaired or detached and that his ability to form intention was grossly impaired.

On crossing examination, Dr. R. Ley noted that dissociative states do not appear in the DSM-IV as each condition by itself does not constitute a disorder. Here Dr. R. Ley drew a distinction between disorders and states, noting that a series of the latter condition could lead to a disorder, but one dissociative state on its own did not allow for a diagnosis of mental disorder. Dr. R. Ley noted that the defense of dissociation is not often raised in court although he has diagnosed the condition before, but very infrequently. While it may have been helpful for Dr. R. Ley to have seen Demers earlier what is important is the subject's recollection of the incident. If the passive side had won the argument in

Demers' mind (resulting in no violence) Dr. R. Ley would still reach the same diagnosis based on the description of what went on in Demers' mind.

While there is no scientific evidence that a person dissociation cannot form intent, these is no evidence that such a person can form intent. Dr. R. Ley noted that "the albescence of evidence is not evidence of absence." Despite the difficulties surrounding this area of psychology, Dr. R. Ley concludes that the legal requirement of intent is not present in a person experiencing dissociative state because they are not in their right mind and are not directing their behavior. Dr. R. Ley respectfully disagreed with the psychiatric assessment made of Demers by Crown psychiatrist Dr. Stanly Semrau.

Testimony of Dr. S. Lohrasbe

Dr. Lohrasbe's testimony was heard by the court on Wednesday, July 17, 1996. He was fully qualified as an expert witness in forensic psychiatry and was able to give his opinion based on a two and a half hour interview with Mr. Demers held on February 10, 1996. Dr. Lohrasbe also based his opinion on the police report, witness statements, a brief psychiatric report by Dr. Semrau, and the audio and written transcripts of Demers' statements to the police. Dr. Lohrasbe was aware of an assessment being done by Dr. Ley, but did not have access to his report before reaching his own conclusions. The general purpose of the interview with Demers was to get a personal and health history and a general clear picture of the patient. From a forensic standpoint it was also necessary for Dr. Lohrasbe to investigate Demers' understanding of the circumstances surrounding the incident and the incident itself. Dr. Lohrasbe prepared a brief report for defense counsel to which he referred occasionally during his testimony.

Dr. Lohrasbe noted that while there is such things as a dissociative states it is an infuriatingly difficult state to describe. Essentially is a disruption occurring within an individual caused by an outside occurrence. Further, it is a disruption in the normal coherent functioning of an individual's mental processes. Normally there is an integration between perception of reality and one's emotions, therefore one's actions make sense, when there is a disruption in this coherence one is in a dissociative state. Such a state is not a specific mental disorder, rather it is a very rare transient mental state that can occur in normal people. Dr. Lohrasbe outlined the distinction between a disorder and a state and noted that to be diagnosed with a disorder there must be a history of ongoing states. The reason for dissociative states not being included in the DSM-IV is that they do not constitute full mental disorder in the same way that a panic attack (a transient state) is not included whereas panic disorder (a mental disorder) is.

Dr. Lohrasbe is generally quite skeptical of dissociative states and has often testified against such a condition on behalf of the Crown. Generally, however, he recognizes that dissociative states can occur in two contexts: after an overwhelming sudden emotional disruption, or caused by trauma spread out over time. In the latter instance the individual's typical ways of coping with the world are undermined by a more chronic slow build-up. It is the second type of dissociative state that occurred in Mr. Demers' case as these was a slow build-up of trauma which was finally triggered on January 2, 1995.

To Dr. Lohrasbe, Demers was obviously chronically depressed because of the many negative incidents with Lee. He experienced a sense of helplessness and felt ashamed and unable to protect his family. Moreover, Demers was unable to express himself in any way to fully ventilate his frustration. An analogous situation is where the "battered wife" is trapped and unable to use her normal coping mechanisms. This was a normal state for Demers to be in under the circumstances.

A person in a dissociative is not, according to Dr. Lohrasbe, in state of delirium. With this notion in mind, he is generally able to remember certain aspects of the incident although his memory tends to be variable. Also, the subject tends to remember things later on although not necessarily in the way they occurred. With later memories, individuals tend to attach meaning to what they are remembering and may fill in the gaps to help themselves understand what took place. For example it is not unusual that Demers could not initially remember the third show by now he does.

The significance of the first fight shows Demers' degree of frustration with the circumstances. He was undeniably frustrated about his own helplessness and the fact that the law seemed unable to help him. After the fist fight, Demers could not understand why things were not going to be over and his tension and depression mounted as a result of Lee's continued threats. On the night in question the conversation that followed Demers' euphoric states was not a normal thought process to have. Demers' description often events in court (as described by defense counsel) was consistent with his statements made in the interview with Dr. Lohrasbe although he did not then use the terms "dominant" and "passive".

In the opinion of Dr. Lohrasbe, Demers was in a dissociative state on the night of the shooting. This opinion is based on a number of factors and is determined after approaching the subject with a good deal of skepticism. Dr. Lohrasbe's

opinion is supported by that fact that he convinced that
Demers is otherwise normal and that the circumstances
were themselves abnormal. Demers' behavior was out of
keeping with his general character as it is very apparent that
he is a peaceful person with high community values. The
lack of a build-up of angry feelings was very striking to Dr.
Lohrasbe. Whereas the common sense approach might be
to say Demers was angry, but there was simply no build-up
here that one would normally associate with rage. After the
shooting Demers became suicidal, a condition that does
not immediately follow a sudden temper flare. There was
also no evidence of anger or rage after the incident when
Demers was arrested as he was most cooperative with
police and did not express anger or hatred towards Lee.

People in dissociative states will almost always express
a state of dual consciousness as is the case with Demers.
The conversation described by Demers is a manifestation
of dual consciousness closely related to depersonalization. It is also significant that Demers described himself as
being detached with one portion of himself observing the
events. Typically dissociative states are caused by unusual
provocation, but here the stimulus was not proportionate
to the response. Instead, the response was an abnormal one
brought about by an abnormal situation. In the dissociative
state, Demers may have been away of some or even most
of his actions, but the whole flow of his consciousness was
abnormal or disrupted. His awareness was certainly not
normal. Being unable to co-ordinate the situation with the
consequences, in Dr. Lohrasbe's opinion Demers was not
capable of intending his actions.

It is not the external appearance that is abnormal in a
person who is dissociating; it is the internal experience
that is abnormal. Various parts of the dissociating mind

are dysfunctioning which to Dr. Lohrasbe suggests that a
person in such a state has no control. Also, whereas voluntariness involves a person being able to perceive things
rationally and to make a choice, a person acting in a dissociative state is unable to act in a voluntary manner. Based
on his interviews with Demers, Dr. Lohrasbe concluded
that Demers' control, intent and voluntariness were all
impaired. Demers was also unable to behave rationally as
he was not in conscious control, i.e. he not fully aware of
his circumstances.

On cross examination Dr. Lohrasbe admitted that he was
sympathetic to Demers' plight but that he did not allow this
to affect his diagnosis as he is trained to consciously avoid
such bias. However, he also noted that he is also human and
that his mind works on subconscious levels he may not be
aware of. Regarding the slight changes in Demers' version
of events (between the police interview and the statements made in court) Dr. Lohrasbe noted that over time
the subject re-visits the experience again and again reinter-
preting the emotional content of the even each time. The
fact that the descriptions are different is not surprising. Dr.
Lohrasbe expressed that in his opinion Demers acted "auto-
matically" with the understanding that "automatic" does
not mean not goal directed. On the contrary, Dr. Lohrasbe
notes that almost all behaviors related to dissociative states
is goal directed behaviors driven by subconscious wishes.
There is nothing bizarre about the external behavior, what
is bizarre is what occurs internally I the mind ot the individual dissociating. Dr. Lohrasbe admitted that he relied on
Demers' version of events as he had not reason to disbe-
lieve him.

The significance of the first tight to Dr. Lohrasbe was that
during that incident Demers may have been angry. He

certainly experienced something entirely different to what he went through during the shooting episode. Demers has a difficulty perceiving himself as an angry person therefore he would not tent to acknowledge that he can be angry. The whole concept of anger frightens Demers and he finds it offensive. During the shooting incident there is no evidence of anger or rage. Demers' experience was one of being in an abnormal state rather than experiencing rage cause by an understandable motive.

Dr. Lohrasbe was questioned in rebuttal and testified that he ruled out malingering in the case of Demers. He testified that he would not have reached the same opinion if he had found Demers to be malingering. Dr. Lohrasbe noted that the dissociative state could also occur in a normal person under the same circumstances as those faced by Demers.

Conclusion

The evidence raised by the testimony of Darwin Demers, Dr. Robert Ley and Dr. Shabarand Lohrasbe concerning this state of mind at the time of the shooting incident was sufficient for the jury to acquit him of all criminal charges. Indeed, the defense of "automatism" or dissociative state negates the *actus reus* of the crime and leads to full acquittal where there is no mental disorder present. Mr. Demers' actions were preformed involuntarily while he suffered from a transient dissociative state brought about by chronic trauma suffered over a three year period. Because of his condition he neither had the capacity to form intent, nor actually formed any intent related to the shooting of Mr. Lee ON January 2, 1995.

Printed in the United States
135770LV00003B/22/A

9 781600 349911